SCHOOL·TIES

BY THE SAME AUTHOR

On the Yankee Station, 1981
A Good Man in Africa, 1981
An Ice-Cream War, 1983
Stars and Bars, 1984

SCHOOL·TIES

TWO SCREENPLAYS:
Good and Bad at Games
· AND ·
Dutch Girls

WILLIAM·BOYD

WILLIAM MORROW AND COMPANY, INC. • NEW YORK

Library of Congress Cataloging-in-Publication Data

Boyd, William, 1952–
School ties.

Contents: Good and bad at games—Dutch girls.
1. Boarding schools—England—Drama.   2. Television
plays—Great Britain.   I. Title.
PR6052.09192S3   1986   791.43'75   86-2523
ISBN 0-688-06568-6

Printed in the United States of America

First U.S. Edition

1 2 3 4 5 6 7 8 9 10

BOOK DESIGN BY LINEY LI

Everyone knows that the only emotion that is fully developed in a boy of fourteen is the emotion of loyalty and honour. For that very reason it is so dangerous. By appealing to it, you can do almost anything you choose; you can suppress the expression of all those emotions—particularly the sexual—which are still undeveloped; like a modern dictator you can defeat almost any opposition from other parts of the psyche. But if you do, if you deny these other emotions their expression and development . . . they will not only never grow up, but they will go backward, for human nature can never stay still. They will, like all things that are shut up, go bad on you.

—W. H. AUDEN
from "The Old School"

A NOTE ABOUT THE AUTHOR

William Boyd was born in 1952 in Accra, Ghana, and was brought up in Nigeria. He was educated at Gordonstoun School, the universities of Nice and Glasgow, and at Jesus College, Oxford. His novel *A Good Man in Africa* won the Whitbread Prize for the best first novel of 1981, and his second novel, *An Ice-Cream War,* was nominated for the Booker Prize in 1982. He has also published a collection of short stories entitled *On the Yankee Station.* His most recent novel is *Stars and Bars.* He lives in London with his wife, Susan.

ABBREVIATIONS IN THIS BOOK

EXT   exterior shot

CU   close-up

VO   voice over

INT   interior shot

POV   point of view

INTRODUCTION

I went to boarding school at the age of nine. This was unexceptional: when I arrived I found boys of six and seven—one even claimed to have been at school since he was five. Some six or seven years later this boy's father died. Somewhat to our surprise, the son expressed no filial grief—he confessed that his father was almost a stranger to him, a genial presence and provider of money whom he met in the holidays.

I was not unhappy to be going away to school. All my coevals in West Africa were doing the same. Expatriate parents were content enough, in those days (1960), with the primary education provided in the ex-colonies but preferred to send their offspring back to the home country when the secondary stage approached. Neither of my parents had been to public school or boarding school and both were unfamiliar with where or how to introduce me to the system. In the event, I went to the same school as a son of close friends of theirs. They had heard good reports of it; I seemed to like the place when I went for my interview one summer when we were back on leave; and, as I was Scots, it was an advantage that the school was in Scotland.

The main school was serviced by two of its own prep schools: a junior, which took boys from six to eleven years old, and a senior, which kept boys until they were thirteen. There was an entrance exam for the main school, but it seemed to me that this was more a device to weed out the seriously dim, the unruly and other undesirables, rather than any real proof of academic merit. In the late 1950s, when I was interviewed and accepted for the school, it was comparatively unknown and inexpensive, distinguished only by its remoteness (in the far north of Scotland), a reputation for its somewhat Spartan life-style (boys wore shorts throughout their school career) and the idiosyncracies of the educational ethos of its founder, who thought a school could be run along principles laid down in Plato's *Republic*.

The junior prep school (now defunct) was housed in a former shooting lodge, a rather magical-looking Scottish baronial building with battlements and turrets. My memories of my year there are almost idyllic. We built forts in the woods, the work was not arduous, the staff were kind, the headmaster prototypically eccentric. Mr. Vaughan, the head, had a shock of white hair, was a bachelor, smoked heavily (Player's Navy Cut), wore brown suede shoes and exuded a certain charming, *louche* sophistication. We sensed, probably from the attention he paid the pretty art teacher, that he was something of a ladies' man. He ran the junior prep school, I imagine, with complacent ease—everybody, boys and staff, appeared to like him. Some years later he took over a house in the main school, but there he was dealing with adolescents brimful of loutish maturity. Beneath his kind, insouciant eyes—and never perceived by him—a state of hoodlum anarchy ruled. It took three years for his successor, a joyless, morose disciplinarian, to lick it back into shape.

I think there is only one prerequisite for success in a prep school (later brains, strength, cunning, power and charisma all play a part) and that is popularity. Academic and sporting achievements at that level are so ephemeral and inconsequential that they carry little kudos. People want to be liked, and if you are, then life is good. The only really miserable boys I saw in those early days were the unpopular ones, and thinking back to it now, it seems to me that they were unpopular because they looked peculiar: Webster had carrot-colored hair and thick black specs; Sedley was unusually olive-skinned. These were the boys we happily taunted (our most severe torment was to gather around the victim and chant "Baitey! Baitey! Baitey!" until they broke down and wept). I was popular enough because I was quite tall and could run fast, though I now recognize that I never made the top rank because I didn't have a nickname. The real stars were called "Ducky" or "Fitzy" or plain "Johnny." Once for a week or so some boys took to calling me a latinate "Boydus" but it never caught on. What made these boys popular—so popular that even the staff addressed them by their nicknames? The answer is, I think, that they were cheerful. After the age of eleven or twelve they seemed to fade out, almost without exception, puberty robbing them of their sunny charm. Somehow their personalities were sufficiently developed at the ages of nine and ten to make them the preteen equivalent of the life and soul of the party, and this was enough to make them everybody's favorites. Indeed, within the small community of the prep school a sort of benign favoritism tends to flourish, rather as I imagine it does in a large family, with no real resentment being expressed by those excluded. For a while—I think as a result of having suffered a very bad dose of chicken pox—I became the favorite of the matron, Mrs. Herrick, a dark, no-nonsense, vivacious woman. She was not the most powerful patron among the staff, but her benevolence did pay dividends.

Every morning we had porridge for breakfast. The school would gather in the assembly room before filing through to the dining room. There would be a prayer, notices would be read and Mrs. Herrick would appear to select the sugar server. This was one of the most coveted jobs in the school (our sweet ration was one Quality Street per day). The sugar-server was required to place one dessertspoonful of brown sugar on every bowl of porridge. The perk of the job w that one was permitted to sugar one's own bowl of porr

13

to one's heart's content. Naturally, friends of the sugar server also benefited. During my reign as Mrs. Herrick's favorite she would come into the assembly room each morning, scan the eager, pleading faces of the boys and then, as if on a whim, select me. This went on for many weeks. I became rather smug and developed a sweet tooth that I have only lately managed to neutralize.

Life at prep school, although unreal, is still an extension of childhood. Consequently our hopes and fears, desires and hatreds, retain some quality of innocence. An enterprising American boy started a dance school where you could learn to twist. It was a huge success. On Saturday mornings you would find thirty or forty little boys "twistin' " with each other in a state of radiant bliss. There was constant heated debate too over the respective merits of the Beatles and the Rolling Stones. As a prefect ("officer") you were allowed to listen to Alan Freeman's *Pick of the Pops* in its entirety on a Sunday evening in a small, dusty boxroom known as "the officers' slum."

If our pleasures were innocent, so was our sex life. Most of our carnal energies were expended in trying to see female members of staff in the nude or, second-best, to catch a glimpse up their skirts. I, and many others, nurtured simultaneous passions for Miss Gray, the art teacher, and Miss Cibber, the music teacher. Miss Gray was tall and languorous with glossy dark hair wound around her head in a Bloomsburyesque bun. She wore purple a lot. Miss Cibber too was dark, almost swarthy in fact, smaller and more sturdy. For ~m she ousted Miss Gray from my fantasies, as her bath- was opposite my dormitory. There was an inch-wide ʔtween the bottom of the door and the floor. We spent ʔnings with our cheeks pressed to the cold linoleum, ɪp through the crack. Miss Cibber's strong legs, ee down, were very familiar. We kept praying ɪd over. She excluded herself from all our af-

fections when she was surprised one day in a passionate kiss
with the English master, a—to our eyes—dull, weak fellow
called Hearn.

At school masturbation was known as "flogging." In those
prepubertal days it was known as having a "dry flog." Maturer
boys were candidly envied. A successful emission was an
event celebrated by the entire dormitory, slippery samples of
semen being passed finger to finger, from bed to bed, as
proof. The most legendary masturbator kept a tomato sauce
bottleful in his bedside locker. There was very little mutual
stimulation. Those boys who crept into other boys' beds were
regarded as mild eccentrics rather than pariahs. Occasionally
we would indulge in a little cabaret with a "striptease night."
Lit by torch beams, boys would shimmy out of their pajamas
and dance naked on their beds. This was regarded as terrif-
ically thrilling and dangerous.

As the time approached for our transfer to the main
school a certain tension became evident in those about to
make the move: from seniors at prep school we were about
to become very insignificant members of a much larger or-
ganism. It seems to me now to be most symbolic that the
rite of passage that marked this alteration in our status—from
child to adolescent, from big fish to little fish—occurred in
our final week at prep school: a private, solemn discussion
with the headmaster on the facts of life.

This chat was known euphemistically as "PD"—"So
and so has PD this afternoon," the whisper would go around.
The initials referred to "pandrops"—a name peculiar to Scotland, I believe—large, round, hard, white peppermints, which
the headmaster would feed a boy throughout his embarrassed
lecture in the belief that the peppermint would prevent any
unseemly arousal. Where he got this notion about the ana-
phrodisiac qualities of peppermint from I have no idea. In
fact the talk itself was sheer tedium. The headmaster began
with: "Have you a sister?"; if the answer to that was negative,

he asked, "Have you ever observed farmyard animals?", then proceeded to a swift discussion of procreation with the aid of crude diagrams on a blackboard. At the end he would ask, "Have you any questions?" This was what each candidate was waiting for. "Candidate" is not a misnomer—questions were swotted up weeks in advance, as if in preparation for a scholarship exam. The whole idea was to remain in "PD" for as long as possible, which, rather than establishing the extent of one's ignorance, was thought instead to confer the glamour of massive virility. Medical textbooks, dictionaries and novels were scoured for sexual arcana. "Please sir, what is tertiary syphilis?" "Sir, how do you do *soixante-neuf?*" It was tacitly accepted that the headmaster was duty-bound to answer everything. It was an opportunity not to be missed. There was a record for longest "PD" (held by him of the tomato sauce bottle—his session had lasted the entire afternoon and was resumed after breakfast the next day), but no one in my year managed much more than an hour.

I have known few buildings as intimately as I knew my house at school; after all, I lived there, day in, day out, for five years. All public schoolboys can claim a similar familiarity, but in almost every case you will find there is no nostalgia for the building itself. Apart from my parental home I have never lived in any one house for longer than three years, but I remember the shabbiest and most transient student bedsits with more affection. It is not all that surprising: the living quarters of your average public schoolboy are at best functional and soulless, and at worst utterly disgusting. If Borstals or remand homes were maintained in similar conditions, there would be a public outcry. I recently visited several famous public schools, and nothing I saw there made me so depressed as the dormitories and the thought that for so many years I had slept so many nights in such dismal and depressing circumstances.

It is, I think, a retrospective revulsion. Adolescent boys are not much preoccupied with personal hygiene, let alone the care and maintenance of their living quarters. But now, when I recall the concrete and tile washrooms and lavatories, the pale-green dormitories with their crude wooden beds, I form a new respect for the resilience and fortitude of the adolescent spirit. Not that the conditions we experienced at school were the worst I have seen. At one school that I visited in Scotland some of the studies were in a converted greenhouse, which the boys had lined with egg boxes in an attempt to provide some insulation. Older buildings in older schools give rise to prospects of damp and decay that are almost Dickensian in their extravagance; the dormitories look like wards in some Crimean war hospital.

Anyway, we were fortunate, if that is the right word, in that our house was newish and made of wood. It looked rather like an army barracks, a large, single-story, frame building, creosoted brown, with a tar-paper roof, constructed around a square, grassy courtyard. There were four very long terraced corridors with rooms off each side. One edge of the square expanded to contain a large locker room, towel and shower room and lavatories; one corner contained the house-master's flat. We ate in a dining room a mile away in the main school, an old, rather attractive, stone manor house whose fine architectural proportions had suffered when a Second World War fire destroyed its mansard roof.

When I arrived at the school, aged thirteen, in 1965 everything about the house was functional and anonymous. The floor, throughout, was brown linoleum; the lampshades were white plastic. Curtains at dorm windows were made from the same drab material. Only in the studies was individual decoration permitted, but as this consisted almost entirely of pictures of women scissored from lingerie and swimwear advertisements, they too had a homogeneous air.

Prospective parents being shown around the house often found the unrelieved wallpapering of brassière and corset ads (interspersed with the odd film star or motor car) something of a shock, and from time to time the housemaster or the headmaster would initiate a clean-up campaign. Shortly after I arrived new regulations were issued. (1) Nudity was banned. Even the most decorous and coy picture from a girlie magazine (or nude mags, nude books, skin mags, as we called them) was not permitted: the pin-up must be clothed. (2) Only three pin-ups were allowed on the wall per person. (3) As a special concession, a fourth pin-up could be kept concealed in a drawer for furtive, private consultation. This is true.

It was vain legislation and constantly had to be reinforced. But as years went by attitudes relaxed, and by the time I left every boy's study looked like a Soho bookshop or soft-porn emporium. Indeed, in terms of fixtures and fittings the history of my house, and of all the other six houses in the school, was one of prettification and improvement. Carpets were introduced; studies were subdivided into cubicles or converted to study-dormitories; painting and wallpapering were encouraged. Taste, as might be expected, was execrable. I remember that in one of my studies we lowered the ceiling by two feet by tacking string to and fro from one wall to another and laying brightly colored crêpe paper on top of the resulting web. In the five years I lived there the character of the house altered by stages from that of some sort of penal institution to that of a moderately prosperous South American shanty town.

Much of this home decorating was subsidized by profits from the house shop. This sold nothing apart from sweets, soft drinks and ice cream and did a roaring trade. It was considered completely normal, in the hour of free time between end of prep and lights out, for one person to consume, say, a liter of Coca-Cola, a packet of jaffa cakes and a packet of digestive biscuits, a Mars bar, a slab of chocolate, some packets of crisps, some strips of licorice and a couple of dozen aniseed balls. Everybody, while his money lasted, seemed to eat constantly. As one rose through the ranks kettles were permitted and, along with them, "brewing" privileges. By the end of my school career I was allowed a toaster. During an average day I might drink between twenty and thirty mugs of instant coffee and eat two large white sliced loaves of bread.

Apart from eating and drinking, the other memory I retain of living in the house was the noise. Certain periods of the day were radio hours. As if on command, dozens of radios and record players would start up. Very little classical music was played. In my era the sophisticated public schoolboy listened to Jimi Hendrix, the Grateful Dead and Cream.

We had a television (black-and-white) in the house common room. Its use was very restricted. Far and away the most popular program was *Top of the Pops*. I am sure its producers have no idea of the profound influence and effect this program had on a generation of public schoolboys. I do not know if it commands the same allegiance today, but I would wager that during the last five years of the 1960s 99 percent of public schoolboys religiously watched the program every week during term time. Everything stopped for *Top of the Pops*. In the entire school nothing moved. In our house sixty boys would somehow cram themselves into the common room to watch it on Thursday nights. And, pathetic as it may seem today, we didn't watch it so much for the music but for the girls in the studio audience. The program was accompanied throughout by the grunts and groans, the whoops and sighs, of group passion. It was, I believe, in every public school in the land, a spontaneous, countrywide expression of terrible lust.

The house was large, but it felt curiously constricted. In the summer one could get outside, but during the winter there was nowhere else to go. Curiously, there was not much traffic between houses, except at senior level. Going into another house in the school was like going into another country, but with the added disadvantage that its inhabitants constantly drew attention to your strangeness. Few events were more unsettling than, as a junior boy, to have to deliver a message to a boy in another house. To be jeered at as an alien was the best you could expect; more often you would be set upon. We were members not so much of different houses as of different tribes. The houses all had different atmospheres, almost different ideologies. One house was corrupt, full of villains; one was full of eccentrics; one house was obsessively self-interested. My house, at least when I first joined it, was very hard.

We had had a succession of popular and ineffectual housemasters. There was no discipline. A new housemaster was strenuously trying to impose his authority. But when he retired to his flat at the end of the day the old regime established itself. The source of the problem was a group of boys in the sixteen-to-seventeen age bracket. They were "bad" in the sense that they had no interest in promotion. In the evenings they terrorized juniors with a kind of candid ruthlessness that I still find chilling to recall. They would roam the junior studies, four or five of these roughs, and beat people up at random, extort money or food, rifle letters and lockers in search of diversion. One felt in a way rather like a medieval peasant during the Hundred Years War: one never knew when another marauding army might march by, randomly distributing death and destruction. It was comparatively short-lived, this period of capricious thuggery, but it provided me with a full catalog of the resourceful cruelties of the adolescent mind. Later the attitude of the house changed to something altogether more genial, but I will always remember my years as a junior, even though I was relatively unscathed. W. H. Auden said he detested fascism because at public school he lived in a fascist state. It is rarely a constant state of affairs, but it is not difficult for private life in a boarding school temporarily to take on certain fascist characteristics. It is the sense of being a victim, or potential victim, that lingers on: the way a house can become at certain moments a place of genuine terror and fear; the way you sacrifice all principles in order to save your skin; the ease with which the ideology of the dominant group seduces you. This is, of course, the private, unadministered life of a boarding house, but in a crucial sense it is *the* reality of being a boarder in a boys' public school. Its opposite is what I call "the prison governor's view of the prison." That has a reality too, but it is for public and official consumption. The inmates experience something entirely different, vital and basic.

If you are lucky, everything changes at school as you grow older, stronger and more senior. Those few to whom this transformation and relaxation does not apply are the saddest products of the system. But for the majority the tenor of the daily round eventually establishes itself as tolerable. However, the last year or two at school, although the most privileged, can also be the most irritating. Most people experience this, and no doubt most people have their own reasons. On reflection, I wonder if my own vague disquiet was not to do with a subconscious reaction against the unrelenting absence of privacy that one experiences as the norm in a boarding school. Looking back at it now, some fifteen years later, I realize that of my nine years at boarding school I actually spent three years on holiday and a full six at school. So for those six years, for example, I usually bathed and showered in the company of eight or a dozen other people; I relieved myself in what was effectively a public lavatory; I dressed and undressed, to order, in a crowded locker room; and, except for my final year, I slept in a room that never had fewer than four people in it and on occasions had fourteen. As a way of life—I am trying to be objective about it —this seems to me to be positively bizarre, not to say noisome and rebarbative. Five years in the same house is not only five years of crowding personalities; it is also five years of enforced proximity to the bodies that accommodate those personalities. The house was not a place for the fastidious.

Few people ever wield power as absolute as that possessed by a public-school prefect. Perhaps if you are an officer in the army, it may be similar, but really I feel it is more akin to something you might encounter in a feudal or totalitarian society, insofar as your power is subject to your whim. Boys may not be allowed to administer corporal punishment, but apart from that the head of house at a public school can—or certainly could—exercise a degree of control over the sixty boys in his charge that, day by day, could be said to be greater even than that of the housemaster.

The power operates on two basic levels. First, you can order people to do things: to shave, to repolish their shoes, to comb their hair, to have their hair cut, to run instead of walk and so on. On the second level you can deprive them of things: their freedom (by enforcing detention), their pleasures (you can forbid them to watch TV or ride a bicycle, reduce their pocket money, confiscate their possessions). A prefect may not be able to beat anybody, but if he works at it, and if the transgressions persist, he could probably have a boy beaten. Conceivably, if the circumstances were right, he could get a boy expelled. It is perhaps sufficient to say that, if he feels like it, a head of house can make the life of anybody in his house absolute hell.

I ended my school career as a head of house—we called them "house helpers." I was not very officious, perhaps lethargic might be more apt, but I don't ever expect to re-encounter that curious sensation of strolling through the house at night while everyone else was working at prep, master of my own territory, knowing that I could go anywhere, search anywhere, order people to do my bidding. It is, for those inclined to exult in it, a heady experience—perhaps not the sort of thing an eighteen-year-old should indulge in.

The occasion when one's power, as it were, stared one in the face was over the issue of haircuts. In those days all young males had long hair, and one of the stigmata of being a public schoolboy was the fact that your hair was so short. Consequently, everyone endeavored to grow their hair as long as possible. The longer your hair, the more "cool" you were. Haircut nights saw the head of house, clipboard in hand, patrolling the studies. His word was law—there was no higher court of appeal. Real dread was in the atmosphere. A local barber visited the house once a fortnight. He had to have heads to cut, a minimum of half a dozen. Who would be chosen? To enter a study was an eerie experience; one might have come to claim hostages or to issue a decimation order. At that moment the power one wielded was palpable.

A side effect of power was adulation. They were not always concomitant, but one usually went with the other. By the reduced standards that operate within any enclosed or confined community it was possible to reach a level of fame or renown similar to that enjoyed by film actors or pop stars in the wider world. These folk heroes had their own fans, even their own imitators. I am glad to say that at my school prowess at games was not the sole route to celebrity-hood. It was the age of student rebellion and we had our own existential heroes. I remember a couple of them vividly. There was Burns, taciturn and poetic. His influence was widespread and was responsible for an improbable Ezra Pound craze that swept the school. Against type, he decided rugby was per-missible and secured a place in the First XV [the first-string team, *XV* referring to the number of players on the field, in this case, rugby, which has fifteen]. But somehow he man-aged to play his rugby in a dissident, rebellious manner too —brooding, never shouting, socks always around his ankles—so it did not diminish his *réclame*. Patmore's hero was Oscar Wilde. He always wore his duffel coat like a cloak and parted his hair in the middle. He would saunter around, carrying a daffodil, with half a dozen acolytes at his heels. I do not know what has become of these two, but from time to time I do encounter other erstwhile superheroes and am always astonished at how bland and ordinary they are, and wonder from where they derived their early renown. The sad thing for these people is that adult life can never duplicate the fabulous triumphs of their schooldays—they peak at age seventeen or eighteen and it is all a long slide down from then on. They are the great reminiscers.

At my school promotion did not bring any great increase in privileges. Everyone wore the same uniform and rank was demarcated only by a silk flash on the left-hand side of the regulation school jersey. A house helper usually got a single study bedroom, and the prefects ("color bearers") enjoyed a more lax routine. Baths were a great luxury. We had two to serve sixty boys, and a house helper's privilege was to order any boy out of a bath and take it as his own. There was always a huge waiting list, and because of the time involved the water was never changed. As a junior I would often step into a tepid bath in which the water was absolutely opaque from the grime of its seventeen or so previous occupants. As I grew more senior so my baths grew clearer. My one decadent luxury as head of house was to order the bell ringer (the boy who woke up the rest of the house) to run me a bath in the morning. It would wait there—unused, steaming, limpid—until I came down to the shower room to claim it.

My own progress to this exalted position was straightforward. I moved up through the various ranks to color bearer, and there I would have stayed had not the head of my house been promoted to head boy ("Guardian"—Plato's *Republic* again) and I was pushed up to fill the vacant role. I do not think, from the official point of view, that I was a very good head of house—I was too lazy to put myself about in the accepted way. My two interests at that stage of my school career were sport and painting, and they, rather than official duties, claimed most of my energies. I was demoted to color bearer for a term for staying out one night during a tennis tour in Edinburgh. An energetic Canadian took over for the interregnum (I was reinstated the next term) and ran the house far more efficiently than I. Fortunately, I was not obliged to move out of my study, so—apart from a certain notoriety—the punishment affected me not at all.

Our school was in Scotland, was in almost every respect a Scottish public school, and yet a strong Scottish accent was a real stigma. Indeed, any regional accent was parodied mercilessly. When people spoke with a strong Scottish accent we would make harsh retching sounds in the base of our throats or emit loose-jawed idiot burblings. Anyone with a Midlands or North of England accent heard nothing but a barrage of "Eee bah goom" and "Trooble at t' mill." We all found the mocking of accents endlessly amusing. This was part snobbery, part self-defense. All public schoolboys have an intensely adversarial relationship with the local population, especially with the local youths. To us the locals were "yobs," "oiks," "plebs," "proles," "peasants" and "yokels." It now seems to me astonishing to recall the patrician venom we would express, like aristocrats faced with imminent revolution—a curious mixture of contempt, fear, guilt and jealousy. They lived, after all, in the real world beyond the school grounds, and however superior we congratulated ourselves on being, there was no escaping the fact that they were freer than we were—and that grated. I am sure that we in our turn were looked on as revolting, arrogant, nasty snobs. By no means a harsh judgment.

We longed to get out of school, but the outside world was both a lure and a taunt. It possessed everything that school denied us and at the same time was a constant reminder of the constraints and abnormalities of the society in which we were confined. Strenuous attempts were made to escape to it.

The easiest way to get there was to be selected for a school team. Because the school was situated so far north a considerable amount of traveling was involved in order to find reputable opponents. Rugby and hockey would take you to Inverness or Aberdeen two or three times a term, and often there were matches in Dundee, Glasgow and Edinburgh. Edinburgh occupied a place in our imaginations rather as Berlin did for poets in the 1930s. It seemed to our impoverished eyes unfailingly sinful and glamorous. To be selected for a rugby tour to Edinburgh meant happy hours in Thistle Street pubs rather than eager sporting challenges.

For the outside world meant alcohol rather than girls. Our stays were usually far too short and too well chaperoned to meet the opposite sex, but there always seemed to be a chance to get drunk. I remember a match in Dundee. A friend, who had left school a term earlier and had gone to Edinburgh Art School, caught the train to Dundee with two hefty overnight bags clinking with booze. After the match we had about forty minutes to drink the lot. The favorite tipple was neat gin washed down with a tot of Rose's Lime Cordial.

Once in the outside world, we tended to band together. This was because we were conspicuous in our uniforms (the authorities had introduced blazer and flannels for exeats to spare our blushes over shorts and knee socks) but also because we were somehow fearful and on edge. The outside world was a welcome source of contraband—pornography, drink, cigarettes—and also, in a sense, fair game. When boys went into towns the shoplifting rate rose alarmingly. In the local Woolworth's two store detectives used to follow one particular boy around. He was the most accomplished kleptomaniac and used to take orders for his Saturday visits. We exulted in our delinquency and bandied legends of epic thefts: a souvenir shop in the Highlands left almost empty when a busload of boys cleaned it out; a boy who dug up copper wires on a nearby RAF station, at one stage blacking out the control tower when he sank his ax into a crucial cable. We would return gleefully to the safety of school, clutching our booty. And yet within the school itself theft was regarded as the most serious and antisocial of crimes—any thief could expect years of excoriation. Two worlds, two sets of standards.

Because of the isolation of the school we did not participate in the life of the local community in any significant way. We were too far away from most boys' homes to make any half-term break practicable. It was not difficult to pass an entire three-month term without ever leaving the school grounds. As one grew older this unnatural segregation became more irksome. My abiding memory of my final two or three years is of a sense of life going on elsewhere. I felt as if I were experiencing a form of internal exile. A few away matches with teams only seemed to sharpen the sensation of missing out, of being bypassed.

The school grounds were capacious, the houses scattered randomly about the estate. I had a friend in a house so far away—over two miles—that I could rarely be bothered to visit him. The scale made it logistically difficult to creep out at night. I believe this is something that happens in most public schools. Here, escape is indulged in for its own sake, not as a means to some illicit end. In our case, and to reduce the risk of discovery, the nearest safe town was eight miles away. To drop from a dormitory window, change into civilian clothes, cycle the eight miles in order to snatch a pint of beer before closing time, then cycle back, was too arduous to make it worthwhile.

The summer was always better. We were very near the coast, and it was not difficult to spend a fragrant afternoon hidden among the gorse on the endless sand dunes, replen-

ished with food and drink bought from stores at nearby car-
avan sites. Summer meant tennis too. The school tennis team
was a member of a league that operated among tennis clubs
in that area of the northeast. We would play against clubs in
places like Inverness, Forres and Fochabers. The great advantage was that these games were played midweek, in the
evening. There was something unreal about these matches.
The six of us in the team would get into a minibus at about
half-past five on a Wednesday or Thursday evening and be
driven to a small county town. There we would be dropped
at the local tennis club. The matches were so regular that
often no master accompanied us. For some reason—perhaps
it was to do with the nature of the league—we often played
against mixed doubles, sometimes against women's teams.
Here, at last, was life as most people led it. I have the most
idyllic recollections of these warm summer evenings: long
shadows cast across the red clay courts, the sonorous "pock,
pock" of the balls in the air, the punctilious courtesy of our
game ("I'm not sure if that was out—play a let!"), a few idle
spectators—two girls, a dog, a ruddy man with a pipe. And
then, afterward, in the small clubhouse, with the glowing,
perspiring wives of dentists and solicitors, all of us still in
our dusty tennis whites, drinking half-pints of ginger-beer
shandy, chatting, laughing in the palpitating dusk. There
was, at least to us boys, a tender, bourgeois eroticism about
these encounters, which was much analyzed on the bus ride
back to school. We often got back late, well after ten, with
the school in bed, all curtains drawn vainly against the sunny
northern evenings. We felt immensely proud of our exclu-
sivity and were the source of great envy. Although I was a
very keen sportsman at school, I find it quite easy to understand why tennis is the only game I play today.

The two main vices were drinking and smoking. Drugs were
taken too, mainly marijuana, but were not anything like as

prevalent as they are today. Smoking was completely banned, drinking almost so. A senior boy might get a glass of sweet sherry or a half-pint of beer off his housemaster if he was very lucky. These drinking restrictions must seem positively antediluvian to today's public schoolboy. I recently sat down to dinner with a housemaster at one of our grandest schools, and the three boys who were invited seemed to drink as much wine as they wanted.

The underworld life of the school, then, was concerned almost exclusively with trying to procure and consume alcohol and tobacco without getting caught. Smoking was the most common. I would say that 95 percent of boys smoked at some stage of their school career, regardless of rank and position. Like any law that is consistently broken by a majority, it became impossible to enforce. Most color bearers —who probably smoked themselves—turned a blind eye. All they asked for was a degree of discretion. I remember my study overlooked a road that led to a nearby wood. Every night after prep I could see the hardened smokers, in all weathers, in all seasons, trudging off for a "drag in the woods." From time to time I'd ask them where they were going, to get the reply, "For a walk." There was nothing illegal about going for a walk. You could always tell the smokers because they chewed gum and reeked of Brut aftershave—a brand unanimously endorsed by schoolboys of my era for its wholly effective smoke-obliterating pungency.

Smoking was cheap, fast and easy to hide. Drinking, possessing none of these attributes, was consequently less frequently indulged in. Usually it took place outside the school grounds. Journeys to and from school at the beginning and end of term were drunken binges. Dances, school celebrations, open days and the like were also opportunities for excess. We tended to prefer neat spirits for speed of effect. I remember after one school dance a friend of mine drank half a bottle of gin. Apart from a euphoric light in his eye he seemed fine when he sneaked back to his dormitory. He was caught the next morning when he woke up in a rank and befouled bed to discover that at some time in the night, without his realizing it, he had not only pissed and shat himself but had also vomited all over his pillow.

There was a certain illicit trade in sex magazines. Scandinavian magazines that showed pubic hair were particularly prized and could be sold for high prices. One enterprising boy who ran the school film society for a term was sent blurry but lurid catalogs from blue-film makers which, as far as we were concerned, were the last word in shocking explicitness. Certain novels were censored: *Lady Chatterley's Lover, The Ginger Man, Last Exit to Brooklyn*. But what was permitted varied from house to house. As a fifteen-year-old I once got into fearful trouble with my housemaster because he discovered me reading Harold Robbins's *The Adventurers*. It was confiscated on the spot. When I boldly asked for it to be returned on the last day of term I was told it had been destroyed.

Apart from thieving, the only genuinely illegal act that occurred with any regularity was joyriding. In my house two boys used frequently to take the assistant housemaster's car out late at night. They would disconnect the mileometer and drive through the dark countryside for an hour or two. The owner of the car never noticed. This was an act of real daring, not to say foolhardiness; the consequences of being caught or of having an accident would have reverberated beyond the school—and yet it was not a rare event. All manner of cars were parked around the school buildings overnight. People would use them. The penalty for this crime would have been instant expulsion, but the staff, I am sure, never suspected that it went on. People could be expelled for theft, sex (homo or hetero) and consistent smoking or drinking or the taking of drugs. Few boys were expelled while I was at school: two went for having sex with school maids (the maids were sacked too); a small clique of drug-takers departed and a few heavy smokers. Boys often left of their own accord. Occasionally there would be "scandals" that made the newspapers—boys vandalized a girl's flat on a rugby tour once, I recall—and also demanded the ultimate penalty. The boy who blacked out the RAF station also made the local newspapers. He was a simple, pale, gangly soul called Clough. He had made hundreds of pounds selling copper and lead pilfered from the air base to local scrap-metal merchants. The school, although properly outraged, had, I think, a sneaking regard for his entrepreneurial drive. His father, who did not want him at home, came up to plead for leniency with the headmaster. Clough's punishment was to dig up all the tree stumps on the estate, a task that occupied all his free time for about two terms.

Swearing was a minor crime too, naturally. It is perhaps worth emphasizing, for anyone who doubts it, that the language of a public school is as bad as that of any army barracks. We employed all the usual four-letter oaths with unreflecting abandon. There were not many nonce words or neologisms in our private language at school for some reason. Perhaps because the school had been founded only some decades before, traditions had yet to establish themselves. At prep school it was pure Jennings and Darbishire—"Vanes," " 'Quis?' 'Ego!,' " "Stale news," "Cave," etc., etc. One exchange that I have never encountered elsewhere I record here for those interested in the folkloric side of public-school life. If you farted ("buffed") everyone was allowed to punch you. However, if you said, "Safeties," before you were discovered, you could foul the air unpunished.

We were obsessed with sex. I know this is true of all adolescent experience, but when I think now of the energy and relentless focus of our interminable discussions about the subject a sort of retrospective lassitude descends upon me, as well as a retrospective anger. *Of course* we talked about sex

—we lived in a freakish, monosexual society. There was a parallel world out there in which the two sexes mingled and interacted and to which entry was denied us. No wonder our curiosity was so febrile and intense—and so destructive. The sexual apartheid to which we were subjected all those years utterly warped our attitudes and precluded us from thinking about girls and women in any way but the most prurient and lubricious. The female sex was judged by one criterion—fanciable or nonfanciable, to put it rather more delicately than we did.

Endless conversation, speculation, fantasizing, poring over sex magazines, fervid masturbation . . . there is something soul-destroyingly monotonous about that facet of public-school life, and one looks back with genuine sadness and weariness at the thought of so much wasted time. But there it was, and at the time it was the favorite hobby. We made the best of our opportunities. Every girl and woman who set foot on the school grounds was subject to the most probing scrutiny—housemasters' wives, innocent secretaries, fond mothers and guileless sisters visiting the school were evaluated with ruthless purpose.

However, the people who bore the brunt of our lewd interest were the maids. These were local girls, I think, and were hired—so public-school rumor famously has it—solely on the grounds of their ugliness. It made little difference. Their encounters with the boys, three times a day at meals, were characterized by a one-sided traffic of sexual banter of the vilest and coarsest sort. Given the opportunity, more daring boys actually molested them—squeezing, pinching, feeling. The girls were remarkably tolerant. I never heard of any boy disciplined as a result of a complaint made by one of them. I think our attitudes to them brought out the very worst in our natures: it was male lust at its most doglike and contemptuous, tarnished further by a brand of willful class disdain and mockery that was almost dehumanizing. I daresay

32

any male sodality—rugby team, army platoon, group of Pall Mall clubmen—can descend to this level for a while, but what is depressing and degrading about the male boarding school is the unrelieved constancy of the tone, year in, year out, for at least five years. It must have some effect.

There was also, it is true, a brand of passionate romanticism about our sexual curiosity that was slightly more amusing. Nobody ever admitted to being a virgin. By tacit consent conversation about the great day was always rather vague and woolly—it was just taken as read that everybody was, well, pretty experienced. There was one boy who made the mistake of confessing, at the age of seventeen, that he had still to lose his virginity. He became a laughing stock in the house. Little boys of fourteen would howl, "Virgin! Virgin!" at him. He came back the next term claiming to have lost it in the holidays, but it was too late. His greatest mistake was to have admitted it—the only honest man among shameless liars. And it was easy to lie—no one could prove that you were not the satyr you claimed to be, come the holidays. It was quite important, however, to live up to your reputation on the rare occasion when the company was mixed. Many a self-appointed stud came to grief at school dances, for example.

There was also the problem of letters. If you boasted of having a girlfriend, some evidence needed to be furnished: a photograph at the very least or passionate letters. We liked our letters from our girlfriends to be as conspicuously feminine as possible—colored paper and envelopes with deckle edges and illustrations and drenched in scent. Post was distributed after lunch in the common room. A letter was inhaled, fondled, groaned and swooned over—exhibit "A" in the defense of your virility.

One boy, a jolly, rowdy person called Dunbar, used to exchange clippings of pubic hair with his girlfriend. In the dormitory the little tufts would be passed round like holy relics. We begged him to go further—the girl was French after all. At our crass, snouty prompting he finally did what we required. Together we composed a touching letter requesting a photograph in the nude. The girl was deeply offended, and the relationship shortly fizzled out.

Some boys, though, had exceptional good fortune. A friend of mine "got off" with the Headmaster's *au pair*, a pleasant Norwegian girl called Ingrid—a fabulously exotic creature to us. Another had an affair with his housemaster's daughter, provoking fraught dilemmas of divided loyalty. The rest of us had to rely on rare opportunities provided by school dances or the biennial Gilbert and Sullivan, when the girls were bused in to play the female chorus.

The school dance was little more than a meat market. By the time the girls arrived all the boys were well fortified with alcohol. At the first slow number they pounced. The occasion degraded everybody. The Gilbert and Sullivans were more fun and more decorum reigned. We were meant to be rehearsing, and we saw the girls quite regularly over a period of a month. Courtship rituals were rather primly observed, and the alliances that were struck up remained for a good while on a rather chaste level—one was often invited to the girl's house for tea on Sunday afternoons to meet her parents, for example. This more sustained contact usually provoked the dormant, romantic side of our nature, and many of us fell deeply in love as a consolation for being denied any physical release. That came, eventually, usually as the dates of the performances approached, a sense of time running out—as with soldiers due to return to the front—affecting both boy and girl. These wistful encounters were not so shaming. They were like any adolescent affair—cute, thrilling, melancholic —a brief foray into real life. They ended after the show as the barriers of the single-sex boarding school were reimposed. The only real victim was the Gilbert and Sullivan, in my memory always appalling, for the simple reason that none of the chorus had joined for the singing.

Every boy who leaves his boarding school has been shaped and formed, like it or not, by his years in that hothouse society. Of course, each individual will be affected to a different degree, but the only effective way of resisting the legacy is to get out early. My generation of schoolboys (class of 1970) was entirely typical not only of every other school but also of the generations that preceded us. We left school as unreflecting snobs—we had a very acute perception of "us" and of "them." "They" were all the yobs, oiks, lefties and deviants who hadn't been to public school. We were also racist, in a robust, cheery, easy-going manner, as the blacks and Arabs at school could testify. "Wog" was the commonest of nicknames and, to us, devoid of pejorative intent. We thought of women quite simply as sexual objects. We were politically naïve—which is to say, knee-jerk Tories of the old squirearchical model. We had our moody rebels, true, but they were influenced by Bob Dylan and Jack Kerouac rather than by any political faith. I knew only one boy at school who claimed to vote Labour—we thought him a ludicrous *poseur* at best, a patent moron at worst. Although most of us had done "A" levels, and the more successful were trying to get into university, we were afflicted with a brand of philistinism that manifested itself as a grave suspicion of "pseuds" or anyone who was too intellectual by half. Also many years of group loyalty, to the school, the house, the team, the power élite, had engendered a mistrust of the individual— indeed, "individualist" was often employed as a term of abuse. The maverick, the odd one out, the not easily assimilable, were to be regarded with caution. Not the best set of values with which to rejoin the world in the last quarter of the twentieth century.

So what happened? I think that, usually, the shock of encountering real life stimulated a hasty course of unlearning. Most public schoolboys have to start a stringent program of reeducation almost as soon as the school gates close behind them. This assumes, of course, that the society in which you are compelled to mix operates under different codes. There are still many walks of life in contemporary Britain where the transition from schoolboy to adult is imperceptible—the attitudes that served you well at eighteen will see you nicely through to retirement.

When I left school I went to live on my own in France for a year. The signal inadequacies of my education swiftly presented themselves to me, and I suppose it was then that I began to look back on the strange institution in which I had spent half my life and to wonder at it.

I often found the focus of my thoughts coming around to one boy, a little younger than me, who had been in my house. This person, a sallow, weak boy called Gibbon, had been hated by everybody, myself included. I have no idea why; he was just very unpopular. He was never really persecuted, just spurned. Sometimes a gang would descend on him, demolish his desk, push him around, but most of the time the punishment was verbal. He was a whipping boy for the house. He appeared to take it in reasonable spirit, was not abjectly miserable, and so there seemed no real cause to change attitudes. He had no friends and walked everywhere by himself. He was so disdained that even other unpopular boys in the house would not associate with him in case the taint was contagious.

My own school career was, in a banal way, a successful one, comparatively untroubled and orthodox, but I kept wondering what it had been like for Gibbon during his five years. When he went home in the holidays and his parents asked him how he was getting on at school, what did he say? And, more important, what effect would those five years have on him as an adult? Would he shrug them off? Struggle on regardless? Carry them like a yoke? When I looked at my contemporaries, boys who had had a far easier time, and saw them, years later, still living in the heavy shadow of their school days, still wrestling with aspects of their personalities that were somehow corrupted, undeveloped or warped, I doubted, somehow, that old Gibbon would be the breeziest and most carefree of fellows.

THE FILMS

The best book on public school is not a novel. It is a work of oral history, the collected testimony of some hundreds of public schoolboys and -girls, called *The Hothouse Society.** To me it is the authentic voice of public school, and I un- hesitatingly recommend it to anyone who wishes to know what it is really like to be at a boarding school. I came across it after a vain search through the pages of English literature for anything about public school that was not some crass glamorization (decent chaps doing down the cads and scoring the winning try in the crucial rugger match) or a homosexual romance. The classics of the public school novel (*Tom Brown's Schooldays, Jeremy at Crale, Stalkey and Co, et al.*) all conspic- uously failed to re-create with any accuracy the realism of life at a single-sex boarding school. Nothing I read bore any relation to what I had experienced.

When I started writing short stories with some regularity in the mid-1970s, one of the projects that I set myself was to write a series of short stories about public school. I finished one of these, called "Hardly Ever," and published it in my collection of stories *On the Yankee Station*, and blocked out ideas for three or four more.

* Royston Lambert and Spencer Millham, *The Hothouse So- ciety* (Harmondsworth: Penguin Books, 1974).

In March 1982 I was approached by Quintet Films and Channel Four and asked if I would be interested in writing an original script for the "Film on Four" slot. There was no brief, other than that the subject should deal with contemporary British life and should not be set abroad.

The idea that I proposed was a film about public school.

Good and Bad at Games is in many ways the product of my speculation about Gibbon's fate, heightened and intensified for legitimate dramatic effect. It is also an investigation of the ways in which one's years at public school can haunt and shape, willed or unwilled, one's adult life.

The film was shot in May 1983 and broadcast in December of that year.

One of my aims in writing the film was to make it as real as possible. Public-school themes are often the subject of television films and series, but these are as lamentably deficient as public-school novels when it comes to giving an accurate impression of the quality of life in the institution. For me, one of the great satisfactions of the film is that I can put my hand on my heart and say, "Yes, this is what it was like." The only real concession we made to public taste was over the language. Steam was rising from the first draft. Most of the vituperation went in order to meet the standards of the IBA [independent watchdog for commercial television, similar to the FCC]; that apart, I feel its documentary status is unquestionable.

In September 1982 I met Sue Birtwistle, an independent producer, who suggested that we try and develop a TV film project together. She suggested a comedy about public schoolboys. I pointed out that I had just finished *Good and Bad at Games* and I wondered if, enthusiastic though I was, the "market" could take another film by me on the subject of public schools. We decided that a comedy was sufficiently discrete, and determined to press ahead.

The idea I suggested took as its starting-point something

I had directly experienced. In 1969 I had gone from school to Holland on a First XI hockey tour. I wanted to write something that not only was funny but also highlighted the sexual conditioning that years of exclusively male company can evolve. *Dutch Girls* is not the story of that 1969 tour, though the laughs, problems and disappointments the boys experience are similar to our own.

The script was initially commissioned by Verity Lambert at Euston Films. But after some delay, caused inevitably by lack of funding, she very charitably permitted us to try elsewhere. London Weekend Television took up the project; it was filmed in November and December of 1984 in Amsterdam and London and was broadcast in the late autumn of 1985.

Both these films appropriated most of the ideas I had formed for my series of public-school stories, a project that I now think is finally aborted. I also feel, though I cannot be sure, that I will not treat the subject directly again. Why have I written so much about public schools? There are two answers. The first is that I spent a hell of a lot of time in one, and I know a lot about it. The second is more problematic. I have an intuition that if you want to understand the mood and character of a nation or race, a very effective shortcut is to study the way they educate their young. I have come to learn a great deal about France and the French, for example, by examining what must be one of the most cut-throat and ruthless educational systems in the Western world. And I am fairly sure that the roots and causes of whatever it means to be "British" lie in this bizarre and powerful system of education that we have created for 5 percent of our privileged young.

Whatever conclusions one may draw from the two films, making them was both hugely enlightening and a great pleasure. For *Good and Bad at Games* I owe a great deal to Jack Gold, Victor Glynn and Mike Ockrent of Quintet films, and to Walter Donohue, then at Channel Four. For *Dutch Girls* I have particularly to thank Sue Birtwistle and also Giles Foster. The excellent cast and crew of both films showed extreme tolerance and good nature toward a writer who persisted in hanging around.

A final word needs to be added. In some respects my generation of public schoolboys was the end of an era. Since then many schools have gone coeducational (my own included), attitudes have altered, rules have been relaxed, restrictions have been lifted. In short, some sort of public-school revolution, it is alleged, has been affected. From one point of view this may indeed be the case, but this applies mainly to the public face of the schools. Everything I have written here and in the films is about the private world of the boarding school, the one occupied, controlled and created by the boys themselves, one to which parents and teachers are denied access. After the broadcast of *Good and Bad at Games* I was invited to several eminent public schools to talk to the boys and, in some cases, girls. It is true that certain aspects of public-school life today were not even dreamed about as possibilities when I was at school. But the film seemed to strike a chord all the same and provoked hot debate. It was clear to me that, beneath the cosmetic alterations, life in a boarding school went on pretty much unchanged.

Good and Bad at Games

A Portman Quintet production for Channel Four. Executive producers: Ian Warren and Tom Donald. Produced by Victor Glynn. Directed by Jack Gold.

NILES	Martyn Stanbridge
COX	Anton Lesser
FRANCES	Laura Davenport
MOUNT	Dominic Jephcott
JOYCE	Frederick Alexander
HARROP	Graham Seed
COLENSO	Ewan Stewart
GIRL	Ceri Jackson
TREGEAR	Philip Goodhew
BOY	Tristram Wymark
GUTHRIE	Rupert Graves

The action of the film takes place at Haig House, Stroud College in 1968 and in London in 1978.

1. EXT. DAY. 1968.

A First XV rugby team preparing for a team photo. Sound very muted. Ad-lib joshing is faintly discernible. The camera moves in slowly as the group squares up. Sounds die away. Arms are folded, chests toughly inflated.
The camera moves in on the seated row. Two-shot of NILES *and* MOUNT *staring seriously into the lens. CU* NILES, *face set, grim.*
PHOTOGRAPHER (*VO*): Right chaps, all set. Smile.
　　(*Hold on* NILES's *furious aggressive face. Click as of camera shutter. Screen goes black.*)

2. TITLE

"Good and Bad at Games"

3. EXT. DAY. 1978.

CU NILES's *face staring into lens, but more mildly and uncertainly. Pull back slowly to reveal another team photograph, ten years on, and this time in motley cricket whites. Some of the faces are the same, notably* HARROP *and* JOYCE *as well as* NILES *and* MOUNT. *This time* NILES *is standing in the back row on the end. He is not wearing whites.*

43

MOUNT *is still sitting in the center. Overall, the expressions are cheerier and more relaxed.*

WOMAN (*VO*): OK, got you.

(*The group breaks up amidst much hearty ad-lib banter.* NILES *is not particularly included in the exchanges. Establish scene. A fairly tatty pavilion and cricket ground somewhere in a London suburb.* NILES *approaches* MOUNT.)

NILES: Hi, Alisdair. Welcome back. How was Belfast?

MOUNT: Glad to be home, Wog. Let's put it that way.

NILES: Yeah.

MOUNT: Good Easter?

NILES: Ooh, fair to middling. (*Shrugs*) Well . . . Pretty hairy, was it? This time?

MOUNT: You know the bloody spud basher, Wog.

NILES: The who?

MOUNT: The spud basher. The Michaels.

NILES: Oh. Oh yeah. God yeah.

MOUNT: Wouldn't exactly say they were my favorite people. Still . . . (*punches* NILES *on the shoulder*) In form, Woggy, I trust. (*Inhales, looks about him*) Christ. A bloody spectator.

Long shot of a small figure in a white mackintosh sitting on a bench on the other side of the field.

4. EXT. DAY. RUGBY PITCH. 1968.

Blast of referee's whistle.
CU of NILES*'s face crushed at the bottom of a collapsed scrum. The scrum gradually sorts itself out, revealing* NILES *clutching the ball to his chest. He gets to his feet, tosses the ball to the opposing scrum half and trots off to take up his position in the three-quarter line. On the way he's stopped by* MOUNT *and there follows a brief whispered conversation. Establish pitch lined with cheering schoolboys ("Come on School!", etc.).*
Hold on small distant isolated figure at one end.

5. EXT. DAY. RUGBY PITCH. 1968.

Shot of COX, *solitary, cold and shivering at the pitch edge. His hair is damp. He gazes blankly ahead. He is approached by* JOYCE.

JOYCE (*seizing the hair in front of* COX's *ear and twisting it*):
     Cheer, Animal. Cheer.

COX (*in agony*): Come on, School!

6. EXT. DAY. RUGBY PITCH. 1968.

CU grass. The amplified sounds of bodily contact, shouts, grunts. The shot of grass is broken by running feet.
Pull back to establish NILES, *with the ball, running furiously for the line. He beats a desperate tackle, sells a dummy to the fullback, then dives beautifully in for a try. Wild cheering from the touch lines.*
CU NILES's *face.*

7. EXT. DAY. CRICKET GROUND. 1978.

Same as Scene 3.
NILES *and* MOUNT *moving toward pavilion. They pass various cars: Golfs, Rovers, a Triumph Spitfire.*
NILES *pauses by the Spitfire. On the rear window is a sticker: "Young Farmers do it in Wellies."*
MOUNT *stops by a Volvo and opens the rear hatch. He sits down and begins unlacing shoes. In the back of the Volvo is his cricket gear and plates of sandwiches covered in self-seal.*

MOUNT: Can you give me a quick net once you're ready,
     Wog?

NILES: Sure.

MOUNT (*preoccupied with cricket boot*): See you in a sec, then.

NILES *moves off, greets a few other teammates. Shout of "Hey,
     Woggy, any chance of a net?"*

NILES *goes into pavilion.*

8. INT. DAY. PAVILION. 1978.

The pavilion is dark. Some wives and players are standing around.
At the rear FRANCES *and another wife flap a linen table cloth over a trestle table.*
NILES *recognizes* FRANCES *as he walks by to enter the changing room, but as she evidently doesn't recognize him he changes his "hello" into a cough.*
FRANCES *looks harassed. She sighs, blows a strand of hair out of her eyes and looks out of the pavilion.*
FRANCES's *POV: long shot out of pavilion across pitch. On the far side a small figure in a white mackintosh sitting alone on a bench can just be made out.*

9. EXT. DAY. PAVILION CAR PARK. 1978.

FRANCES *and* MOUNT *at the rear of the Volvo. In the background we see* NILES *emerge from the pavilion wearing whites.*
FRANCES (*quietly*): If you won't move how am I meant to get the fucking sandwiches out?
MOUNT: Listen, you—
NILES: Ready, Alisdair?
MOUNT: Great, Wog. (*Gets to his feet. To* FRANCES, *softly*) Bitch.
    (FRANCES *seizes two plates of sandwiches, her face set.*)
NILES: Hello.
MOUNT: You know Wog, don't you, darling? Wog Niles. From School.
NILES: Yes, we—
FRANCES: I don't think so. Hello. Listen, Alisdair, do you want me to set these sandwiches out now or wait a bit?

MOUNT (*moving off to nets, swishing bat, calling over his shoulder*): Christ, just stick them on the table. They're only sandwiches. Come on, Woggy.

NILES: See you later. (*Trots off after* MOUNT.)

CU: FRANCES's face.

FRANCES (*quietly*): Stick them up your bum, you big bloody shit.

10. INT. DAY. SHOWER ROOM. 1968.

Seven or eight boys under the showers. Room thick with steam, noise and general elation. Two or three sing: "The hairs on her dicki-di-do hung down to her knee."

NILES *appears at door to a great shout of acclaim. Cheers of "Woggy!"*

NILES *shakes fists above his head like a champ, hugely pleased. There are two filled baths against a wall.* MOUNT *sits in one of them. The baths are overflowing with brackish soapy water.* MOUNT *gets out.*

MOUNT: Here, Wog. You can have my bath.

NILES: God, thanks, Mount.

NILES *gets into the filthy bath.* MOUNT *looks on.*

MOUNT: Good game, Wog. Bloody good.

NILES (*overjoyed*): Bloody good. (*Throws back head and lets out a bellow of elation.*)

11. EXT. DAY. CRICKET PITCH. 1978.

NILES *batting. He hits a four. The ball crosses the boundary near the* SPECTATOR, *who lethargically retrieves it and throws it badly back to a fielder.*

Scoreboard: NILES's *score advances to 67.* NILES *takes guard, and looks about him, checking the field placing.*

NILES's *POV: the bench where the* SPECTATOR *was sitting is now empty.*

12. INT. DAY. TOWEL ROOM. 1968.

*The towel room gives on to the shower room. It's a room lined
with hot pipes from which the boys' towels hang. Two large
laundry baskets are provided for soiled towels. Sounds of singing
from the shower room—"dicki-di-do" again.* NILES *appears in the
shower-room door, obviously greatly enjoying himself. Steps into
towel room and begins to dry himself.*

COX *emerges from the shadows in one corner.*

COX: Great try, Niles.

NILES (*surprised*): What? Christ!

COX: Great try.

NILES: What the hell do you want?

COX: Nothing.

NILES: Good.

COX: I just said . . . I thought it was a great try today.
  Really great.

NILES: Well . . . Just bugger off.

COX (*unmoved*): OK, Niles.

NILES (*savagely*): Just bugger off, you frigging weirdo!

13. EXT. DAY. CRICKET PITCH. 1978.

NILES, *out, leaving the field to applause from the wives and
teammates gathered outside the pavilion.*

14. INT. DAY. PAVILION. 1978.

NILES, *unpadding, doesn't see* FRANCES *who is sitting beside the
spread tea table smoking a cigarette and reading a paperback.*

FRANCES: Is it nearly over yet?

NILES: Oh! Christ, I didn't . . . No, not yet.

FRANCES: Oh God. Are you winning?

NILES: Bit early to tell. Made a good start though.

FRANCES: Oh God. (*Returns to her paperback.*)

48

15. EXT. NIGHT. STREET OUTSIDE CRICKET PITCH. 1978.

Long shot of NILES *leaving alone. Pull camera back to expose the
white-mackintoshed* SPECTATOR *watching him. Cut to:*
NILES (*waving*): Bye. See you next week. (*No reply so he
    shouts*) Bye!
    (*Pauses. Still no response. Walks slowly to the bus stop.
    Cut back to* SPECTATOR'*s face. The* SPECTATOR *is* COX.)

16. INT. NIGHT. BOOT ROOM. 1968.

CU COX'*s face, deeply shadowed, inhaling strongly on a
cigarette stub. He is crouched in the dark alcove of the boot room,
a cavernous labyrinthine cellar lined with shelves—floor to ceiling
—containing all manner of boots and shoes. There are also racks
for hockey sticks, broken-down gym equipment, etc.*
COX *stubs out cigarette and drops it in his pocket. He removes a
small bottle of Brut aftershave from another pocket and applies it.
Then he puts a piece of chewing gum in his mouth.*
*He moves out of the shadows and we see that he is in dressing
gown and pajamas. He stands perfectly still for a while listening,
before moving cautiously across the boot room floor.*

17. INT. NIGHT. CORRIDOR, HAIG HOUSE. 1968.

*Shot of a long moonlit featureless corridor, off which there is a
flight of steps descending to the boot room.*
The house is totally quiet, the corridor deserted.
COX *appears at the top of the boot room steps and peers into the
corridor.*
The corridor from COX'*s POV: Suddenly all the lights go on and
a door opens at the far end.* COX *jerks back.*
MOUNT, JOYCE, NILES, COLENSO *and* HARROP *spill into the
corridor.*
COX *flattens himself against the wall on the boot room stairs.*

CU cox's *appalled and terrified face as we hear the muttered conversation and the tread of the others approach and then go by him.*
cox *slumps for an instant, and then scurries off.*

18. EXT. NIGHT. STREET. 1978.

NILES *walking up street toward his flat.*
NILES's *POV: sees two Rastafarians unpacking a very beaten-up van. He pauses. One* RASTAMAN *looks up, sees* NILES *staring and gives a wave.*
The two RASTAMEN *take enormous loudspeakers from the van and carry them into* NILES's *building.*

19. INT. NIGHT. STAIRS IN NILES's BUILDING. 1978.

NILES *ascending stairs with kit bag.*
The two RASTAMEN *ascending in front of him. They stand aside to let him go by.*
NILES *has a frozen smile on his face.*
FIRST RASTAMAN (*genially*): Hi. You live upstairs?
NILES: What? Oh, yeah. Sure.

20. INT. NIGHT. NILES's FLAT. 1978.

Establish NILES's *flat. Scruffy rented accomodation only scantily personalized with a few books, some scattered magazines—some of the* Penthouse, Mayfair *variety.*
On the mantelpiece is a small silver cup. On a table there are some photographs: a family group, NILES's *parents and the team taken in Scene 1. There is a small portable typewriter on a table by the window, a record player and some stacked LPs.*
NILES *comes in, throws down gear and goes to stand by window looking down into street. He doesn't switch on any lights.*
Pan round room to photo. Pan back to NILES. *Suddenly the sound*

of reggae can be heard from below, a persistent thumping bass.
NILES *moves from window, selects a record and puts it on his
record player. It is "Badge" by Cream.
He sits down at the table. Leans back, pinches bridge of nose.
Leans forward, rests head in hands. Hold for a couple of beats, as
he listens to the music.*

21. INT. NIGHT. NILES'S STUDY. 1968.

NILES *at his school desk in exactly the same position. Frowning.
On the desk a copy of* Julius Caesar. *In front of* NILES *an open
notebook with "Julius Caesar" written at the top of the page.
At four other desks in the study are* MOUNT, JOYCE, HARROP
and COLENSO. *The walls of the study are covered with pictures of
women, scissored from lingerie and swimwear ads in magazines.*
MOUNT *and* JOYCE *are working.*
HARROP *is staring at the pictures on the wall.*
COLENSO *is peering into a small mirror propped on his desk and
practicing different ways of combing his hair.
The study is crudely and brilliantly lit, as are all the school
scenes.
It is totally quiet.
Then* COLENSO *lifts a haunch and farts loudly. Mutters of
"God" and "Bloody hell" from the others.*
COLENSO *sits back and sniffs the air.*
HARROP (*neutrally*): You disgusting bloody vermin,
    Complex.
COLENSO (*ignoring him*): Whew, that's a beauty.
    (*Pretends to usher the farty air in* JOYCE's *direction*)
    Have a whiff, Bog Door.
JOYCE (*amiably enough*): Keep your bloody farts to yourself,
    you revolting fat pervert.
    (*Silence for a while.*)
HARROP (*standing up*): I'm off for a wank.
MOUNT: Prep's nearly over.

HARROP: Oh. Right.
(*Sits down and resumes staring*)
But I'm desperate. (*No response from the others.*) I've
already had three. (*Faintly worried expression.*)
NILES: What? Today?
HARROP: Yeah.
COLENSO: Jesus.
NILES: Save it for the dance.
MOUNT: Are you going, Wog?
NILES: Yeah . . . Well, I put my name down.
HARROP: You sly bastard!
JOYCE: I thought it was only powers who could go.
And 6A.
COLENSO: 6A are a load of sheep this year.
MOUNT: But, Christ, you weren't going to go on your
own, Wog, were you? Surely.
NILES: Um no. Oh no. I didn't really think. I mean, I'd
rather go with you lot. But Joyce said you didn't
want to.
JOYCE: I bloody did not.
COLENSO: You bloody did.
MOUNT: Christ, you might have checked, Wog.
NILES: I was going to. Honest. It's just that I heard
someone say 6B had a chance this year. No one in 6A
wanted to go. So I just . . .
COLENSO: It's like I said: 6A are a load of sheep. (*Bleats*)
"I don't want to go to a dance. There will be girls
there."
HARROP (*throwing his head back*): Baaahh. (*Bleating like a
sheep.*)
(*General amusement at this.*)
MOUNT: Keep it down, you guys.
(*They return to their work for some moments.*)
NILES: How do you spell "conspicious"? (*Looks at his essay*)

"Caesar's wife, Calpurnia, is conspicious by her absence."

HARROP: Conspic*uous*. "Conspicuous," you dense bloody cretin. Conspicuous!

MOUNT: C-O-N-S-P-I-C-U-O-U-S.

NILES (*embarrassed*): Thanks.

COLENSO (*amused*): "Wog Niles was conspicious on the rugby field last weekend."

JOYCE: "Niles's essay on *Julius Caesar* was conspiciously inferior."

HARROP: "Bog Door Joyce possessed a number of conspicious pus-filled yellow-headed spots on his fat face."

(*Laughter.*)

JOYCE (*nettled*): Sod off, Harrop.

HARROP: Woho! He's sensitive, is he? Oh *gosh*.

COLENSO: Look, what about this bloody dance then? We can't let Wog go on his own.

MOUNT: We should all put our names down. All of us.

COLENSO: Good thinking, Batman!

HARROP: Yeah, but what will the slags be like? That's what I want to know. Will it be worth it?

JOYCE: Sex-starved. As sex-starved as you.

COLENSO: Yobesses. "Ee by goom." "Trooble at mill."

HARROP: Just as long as there's one with big tits.

JOYCE (*sardonically*): Oh yes. Tit-man Harrop.

HARROP: Bum-bandit Joyce.

JOYCE (*false smile*): Shove it, Harrop.

HARROP (*cheerfully*): Up yours, mate.

(*This exchange is interrupted by a bell, followed by a shout: "End of prep!" There is an immediate outbreak of noise from beyond the study: shouts, running feet, pop music. Another bell goes: "Shop!"*)

I think I will go for that wank after all. (*Leaves.*)

(NILES *throws his pen down. The others all take food—large quantities of biscuits, sweets, bottles of Coke and lemonade—from their desk cupboards and begin eating and drinking.*
There is a knock at the door.)

MOUNT (*shouts*): Yes!
(COX *comes in. He carries a broom, dustpan and a black plastic sack.*) What do you want, Animal?

COX: Study duty, Mount.

JOYCE: Well get a move on, Animal.
(*During the subsequent conversation* COX *moves nervously about the study sweeping and dusting and emptying wastepaper baskets. He is evidently riven with apprehension but the others behave as if he is invisible.*)

NILES: Didn't do a bloody thing. Julius bloody Caesar. "What were Brutus's motives in betraying Caesar?" Did you do that question, Complex?

COLENSO: Yeah. A breeze.

NILES: Well, what's the answer then? Why did he do it?

COLENSO: Jesus, Wog, it's so bloody obvious.

NILES: Is it?
(*Looks back at his book*)
I can't see why.

COLENSO: Why does anybody betray anybody else?

NILES: But I thought they were meant to be friends, comrades in arms, that sort of crap.

COLENSO (*patiently*): But that's just it, Wog, don't you see?
(COLENSO *looks at* MOUNT *behind* NILES's *back. He places his palm on the side of his face, looks stupid, rolls his eyes and mimes a "duhh" sound.*)

JOYCE: Shut up talking about bloody work, will you? Prep's bloody over. (JOYCE *puts a record on a battered record player. "Badge" by Cream. He picks up a tennis racket and, holding it like a guitar, plays along with the record quite unselfconsciously.*

COLENSO *gets up and dances across the room to* NILES*'s desk where he helps himself to a biscuit and starts reading* NILES*'s essay.*
A sort of lassitude descends on the four as they eat and listen.)
NILES: I love this bit.
(Guitar break in "Badge" JOYCE *writhes over his tennis racket.)*
Should I play Costas at scrum half?
MOUNT: He's a spastic.
NILES: I know. But there's no one else.
MOUNT: What does it matter? They're all spastics. It's a wet-pants spastic team.
JOYCE *(putting down racket)*: Where do these girls come from, anyway?
MOUNT: What girls?
JOYCE: Who'll be at the dance.
COLENSO *(returning to his desk)*: A place called St. Margaret's *(puts on Yorkshire accent)* "Co-ledge for t' educashoon of yoong ladies."
MOUNT: How old are they?
COLENSO: Our age. No, perhaps a bit older.
NILES *(impressed)*: Jesus.
MOUNT: Shit. Think of it. Bloody tarts. Bloody queuing up for it.
JOYCE *(troubled)*: Yeah. Jesus.
COLENSO: Jesus H. Christ.
(Pause.)
JOYCE *(seriously)*: Have you got somebody . . . I mean, is there somebody—not somebody you've ever actually shagged—but somebody who, if you ever wanted a shag, would let you? Who, you know, you could just go to and shag?
MOUNT *(thinking)*: Well . . . yes. Yes, I have. There is someone.

JOYCE: Complex?

COLENSO: No problem.

JOYCE: Wog?

NILES (*a bit edgy*): Um . . . Yeah. Yeah. Now that I come to think of it. Mmm. Yeah, there is someone . . . I mean, I've never actually shagged her. But, if I wanted to I know I could.

MOUNT: Exactly.

(*Pause.*)

JOYCE (*very thoughtful*): It's good to know that, isn't it? I mean, it's good to know that . . . if you ever . . . (*trails away.*)

COLENSO: The girl I'm thinking of is the one I met last summer. Véronique.

(*French accent*)

Véronique. Véri nice nickères. She promised to send me some cuttings from her pubes.

MOUNT (*incredulous*): Come off it!

COLENSO: No, it's true. Really. We said we'd exchange clippings. A sort of memory of last summer. I've already sent her an envelope full of mine.

JOYCE (*genuinely appalled*): That's *bloody* revolting!

(MOUNT *gets up, moving to* NILES's *desk, and crosses* COX's *path.* COX *stops dead, looking at the floor.* MOUNT *passes by.*)

MOUNT: I thought you were looking a bit patchy. A big mangy. I thought it was some disgusting pox. Can I have a swig, Wog? (*Drinks* NILES's *Coke.*)

COLENSO: The trouble is, I think I've sent it to the wrong address. She gave me two addresses and she said whatever I did I mustn't send lustful letters to one of them. Unfortunately I've forgotten which one . . . (*Laughter.*)

MOUNT (*laughing*): Imagine it. Christ, at breakfast. (*French accent*)

"What eez zis lettère from Angleterre? Show me, Véronique."

COLENSO (*piping French accent*): "Oh. Eeet eez only some pubique air from my boyfriend, papa."
(*Much ribald laughter. CU* COX, *impassive, pretending not to have heard.*)
Chuck us a biscuit, Wog.
(NILES *picks up a biscuit and aims.* COX *is in the way.*
NILES *throws and* COX *ducks out of the way. For an instant their eyes meet. This casual action should somehow seem to be significant.*)

MOUNT: Did you see what bloody Twisted was wearing in Latin today? A dirty little yellow bow tie.

COLENSO: Typical. I think that man's trying to prove he's got some personality. He's so bloody bourgeois, that guy. Total bourgeois. Makes me want to boke.

NILES: It's probably a present from Mrs. Twisted, trying to improve him. She's up the spout again, you know. Saw her in chapel last Sunday. (*He holds an imaginary belly out in front of him.*)

MOUNT (*disgusted*): Again? Jesus.

COLENSO: God, she's ugly, that woman. Seriously ugly.

MOUNT: Must be overdue for a rebore. How many's that?

JOYCE: Four. Four Twisted brats. Breed like rabbits.

MOUNT: He's a bloody left-footer, what do you expect?
(HARROP *comes in, sees* COX.)

HARROP: Who's a bloody left-footer? (*To* COX) What are you doing in here, Animal? Vermin aren't allowed in here.

COX (*mumbling*): Sorry, Harrop. Wasties, Harrop.
(COX *goes to* MOUNT's *desk for the last waste-paper basket.*
MOUNT *is sitting on his desk, his feet on his chair.*
COX *busies himself at his feet, spills some paper from the basket, scrabbles it desperately into his sack.*
MOUNT *is oblivious.*)

MOUNT: Twisted is. And he's buggered up his rhythm method for the fourth time, Wog says. Stick that record on again, will you, Bog Door?

JOYCE (*to* HARROP): Feel better, Harrop? Feel more at ease with yourself? Sort of drained?

HARROP (*giving* JOYCE *a V-sign*): By the way, I've just signed us all down for the dance.
(*Rubs hands together in simulated lecherous glee*) Two weeks on Saturday, my friends! (*Punches air.*)
(*Shouts of approval from the others.* JOYCE *puts on* "Badge."
The opening chord rings out loudly.
Everybody sings along, plays imaginary guitars, drums, etc.
COX *slips unobtrusively out of the door.*)

22. INT. NIGHT. NILES'S FLAT. 1978.

NILES *staring out the window, looking down on the street.* "Badge" *is still playing.*

23. NIGHT. STREET OUTSIDE NILES'S FLAT. 1978.

NILES's *POV: Figure in white mackintosh walks quickly past.*

24. INT. DAY. NILES'S OFFICE. 1978.

NILES *in shirtsleeves sitting at a desk in a small shabby open-plan office. Various accoutrements—cheap furniture, whimsical coffee mug, girlie calendar—establish his position as lowly managerial. The place is very depressing.*
NILES *picks up phone. Puts it down. Picks it up again and dials.*
NILES: Ah, hello. Could I speak to Mr. Joyce please . . .
Yes, Joyce, Mr. Joyce. Oh, um, say it's Mr. Niles.
N-I-L-E-S. Niles. (*Pause.*) Hello, Jerry? Jerry, it's
Quentin here. Quentin Niles . . . Quentin Niles.

(*Articulates*) Quen-tin Nigh-ills . . . *Wog.* Yes! Hi,
hi . . . yes, ha-ha, I know what you mean. No, don't
give it a thought . . . Look, ah, Jerry, I was
wondering if we could get together for a chat
sometime . . . No, actually it's nothing to do with the
team . . . It's to do with me. l thought perhaps if you
had a few minutes . . . Lunch? Well . . . Great, if
you're . . . Well yes, yes . . . (*patently grateful*)
Marvelous, great . . . The what? Simpson's . . . In the
City. Don't worry, I'll find it . . . Half-twelve,
Thursday. Fine with me. Couldn't be better . . . See
you then. Marvelous, marvelous. Bye, Jerry, thanks
again . . . Bye.
(NILES *sitting at his desk, a look of baffled gratitude on his
face. Wipes his palms on his thighs.*)

25. INT. DAY. SUPERMARKET. 1978.

NILES *shopping listlessly, throwing prepacked foods into his
trolley. He examines various packs of Vesta curry.
Shot of* NILES *from the back. A hand tapping him on the
shoulder.* NILES *turns. Sees* COX *pushing an empty trolley.* COX
*is wearing his white mac. Also has a feeble moustache and
longish lank hair.*
COX: Hello, Niles.
NILES: Um, I'm sorry, I—
COX: Sorry. Hello, "Wog."
NILES: Just a—
COX: Still ringing no bells? I'm Cox.
NILES: There must be some mistake.
COX: No mistake. I'm Cox. From school. I think you'll
   probably remember me as "Animal." Or "Germ." Or
   "Dog."
NILES (*dubiously*): Oh.
COX (*eerily relaxed*): Yes, that's me. "Animal" Cox. From

school? Think of the boot room, that'll help.

NILES: Ah. Yes . . . Well, how are you? I, um, didn't know you lived around here.

COX: I don't.

NILES: Oh. Just passing through. Quite a coincidence . . . Us meeting.

COX: No.

NILES: What?

COX: No coincidence.

NILES: Oh.

COX: I wanted to see you.

NILES (*astonished*): Me?

COX (*with heavy irony*): Shall we repair to an adjacent hostelry? Partake of some mild alcoholic libation?

26. INT. DAY. PUB. 1978.

The pub is almost empty. "Time" has been called.
NILES *and* COX *sit at a table, two near-finished pints in front of them.* COX *laboriously rolls a tiny thin cigarette. He has removed his mac; the clothes he is wearing look poor and seedy.*
NILES *sits with growing impatience, his arms folded.*
COX *lights up and exhales confidently.*

NILES: I'm sorry. What was it you said you did?

COX: I'm a journalist. An investigative journalist.

NILES (*highly skeptical*): An investigative journalist. I see. What paper?

COX: I'm free-lance. Just at the moment. (*He taps the side of his nose.*) It's often the best way.

NILES: Is it?

COX: I'm working on a rather biggish story at the moment. Could be rather important. Repercussions. (*Waggles hand.*) But rather dodgy, if you know what I mean. Rather dodgy.

NILES: What's that then?

COX: What?

NILES: The story you're meant to be working on.

COX: Funny you should ask.

NILES (*exasperated*): Is it?

COX: Yes. Because you might just be able to help me out.

NILES: You don't say?

COX: Yes, I do. You might be just the person in a position to do me a good turn.

NILES: What's it about, this story?

COX: It's about Northern Ireland.

NILES: Northern Ireland? Me?

COX: To be more precise, it's about British troops in Northern Ireland. To be even more precise, it's about certain British officers in Northern Ireland.

NILES: I'm afraid you're barking up the wrong lamppost. I don't know anything about Northern Ireland.

COX: Don't you?

NILES: I don't want to know anything about it either.

COX: I see. (*Relighting cigarette, then changing subject*) I've been out of the country for a year or two. Beirut, the States. You may have seen some of my articles. And uh, before that, after leaving school, I was pretty sick for a while. Pretty ill, what with one thing and another. (*Smiles.*) Touch and go.

NILES: Uh-huh.

COX: Yep, "Touch and go." Odd expression that, don't you think? Touch and go. Rather like another one— been puzzling me lately. "Common or garden." As in "Common or garden intelligence." I know what common intelligence is, but what the hell is garden intelligence? I don't suppose you can help me out on that one, can you?

NILES: Sorry. I haven't the faintest. I don't usually think about these things.

COX: You couldn't say you were the world's most curious

person, were you? Don't want to know about Northern Ireland. Unconscious of the nuances of the English language . . . Still, different strokes and all that. Look, there was another one. Different strokes for different folks. (*Looks at cigarette, then holds it up*) I'm meant to be giving these things up. Doctor's orders. That's why I'm "rolling me own." The theory is that you get so pissed off making the bloody things you stop. (*Pause.*) Or else go back to packs . . . I picked up the habit at school. Been a heavy smoker since the age of fourteen . . . You don't smoke, do you?

NILES: Me? No.

COX: No. Still keeping fit, eh? Still play a bit of sport, do you?

NILES: Well, mainly in the summer. Cricket most weekends. For the Wanderers, you know. Bit of rugby, squash in the winter.

COX: You were good at games, weren't you? I remember. (*Pause.*) So. You play a bit of cricket for the Wanderers, then, do you?

NILES (*suddenly realizing*): Christ. You're the spectator.

COX (*delightedly*): Yeah. That's me. Doing my ground work. Research. Background, we call it. (*Taps side of nose, and relights cigarette.*)

NILES (*puzzled*): Yes. Well, look, um . . . (*looks at watch*) I think they want us out of here and in any case I'd better be running along. Nice to have, um, you know—

COX (*suddenly hostile*): You have absolutely no idea what my first name is, have you? Absolutely no bloody idea at all. You saw me every day for five years and you haven't the faintest notion what my Christian name is. Bloody hell. Have you?

NILES: Christ, it's just not one of those things I—

COX (*suddenly calm*): It's John.

NILES: Right, *John*. Nice to see you again after all this time.
(*Gets up and picks up his carrier bag, which drips
copiously, all his frozen food having defrosted.*)
Hell!

27. INT. DAY. NILES'S FLAT. 1978.

Door opens and NILES *enters with dripping shopping bag,
obviously in a black mood.*
A few steps behind him comes COX.

COX: So this is your "pad."
(NILES *goes wordlessly into the kitchen.*
COX *prowls around the sitting room, poking about, picking
things up. Takes* NILES'S *cricket bat from the kit bag and
plays some inept-looking strokes.*) Very nice indeed.
(*Raising his voice*)
Your place. Very "swish."
(*Pause, then still in a loud voice*)
You haven't got a cigarette, have you? I mean a
proper one. It's just that I can't be bothered spending
ten minutes making something that takes thirty
seconds to smoke.
(*Laughs to himself.*)

NILES (*coming in, wiping his hands on a dishcloth*): I told you, I
don't smoke. (*Takes bat away from him and replaces it in
the kit bag.*) Look, Cox—John—I've got to be off in a
minute or two.

COX: Save the food?

NILES: Just about.

COX: Good . . . Playing cricket, are you?

NILES: Yes.

COX (*looking skeptically at watch*): I see. Playing for the
Wanderers?

NILES: Yes.

COX: Who against?

NILES: Old Carthusians, I think.

COX: Ah. The "Old Carthusians." Will Mount be playing? "Captain" Alisdair Mount?

NILES: Alisdair? Yes. Why?

COX: Just back from Ulster, is he?

NILES: You should know, you've been watching the games. (*Pause.*)

COX: Are you still friendly with Mount?

NILES: Look, what is this? Yes I am. He's . . . I suppose he's my oldest friend.

COX: "Oldest friend." I see.

NILES: Why do you want to know?

COX: Because I'm very interested in Captain Mount. Very interested in his career. In the army. (*Tapping the side of nose.*) From a professional point of view, if you know what I mean.

NILES: No, I don't know what you mean. What the hell are you talking about?

COX (*briskly*): I'll tell you exactly what I'm talking about. Why don't you come and have dinner at my place next week?

(*CU:* COX's *odd smiling face.*)

28. INT. NIGHT. BOOT ROOM. 1968.

Stark pools of light and opaque shadows.
COX *emerges from shadow and stands in a wand of light for a second—motionless, expressionless.*

29. INT. NIGHT. COX's STUDY. 1968.

A large and shabby study with eight desks upon which are flimsy towering partitions and shelving systems made from orange boxes and the like.

64

Four BOYS *sit expectantly at their desks.*
Another stands at the door looking down the passageway. This
boy holds a piece of string in his hands which leads to one of the
taller desk constructions.
BOY: Here he comes.

> (*The* BOY *shuts the door and slips the end of the string over*
> *the door handle.*
>
> *A few seconds later* COX *comes in, swings the door open and*
> *sees his entire desk construction tumble to the ground. Great*
> *hilarity from the others.*)

COX (*softly*): You filthy shags.

> (COX *goes over to his desk and the rubble surrounding it.*
> *He picks up one or two things. His face is expressionless.*)

FIRST BOY: What's the matter, Animal?
SECOND BOY: Shouldn't be so bloody careless, Animal.

> (*General laughter.* COX *turns on his heel and runs out of the*
> *room, followed by the others, whooping and mocking. Cut*
> *to Scene 30.*)

30. INT. DAY. LAVATORY. 1968.

COX *sitting on WC in tears.*
From his POV we see mirrors being thrust under the door, faces
peering over the top of the partition. Chants of "Animal's
crying, Animal's crying," "Aw, diddums," etc. From this din,
cut to Scene 31.

31. INT. DAY. CITY PUB. 1978.

NILES, *his hands full of drinks, struggling through a noisy mob of*
young, dark-suited bankers and stockbrokers.
Joins HARROP *and* JOYCE.
NILES *is dressed wrongly—a light brown suit—and has spilled*
some of the drinks on it, causing a prominent stain. He looks out
of his depth and ill at ease.

65

JOYCE: Thanks, Woggy. Cheers.
HARROP: Mmm. Cheers, Wog.

32. INT. DAY. SCHOOL DINING ROOM. 1968.

Same immense noise, babble of conversation.
A bell rings, silence, the boys all gather behind their chairs.
VO grace is heard: "For what we're about to receive, may the
Lord make us truly thankful."
The last words are drowned in the noise of a hundred chairs being
dragged back and of interrupted conversation being resumed.
Dishes and soup are carried from serving trolleys by junior boys
and are placed at the heads of tables.
MOUNT is serving at one table. He is flanked by JOYCE and
NILES. COX is seated further down.
MOUNT: Cox, go and open that window down at the
    bottom, will you?
    (COX *complies.*
    MOUNT *serves up a bowl of soup and as it's passed down*
    the table to COX's *place, everyone spits in it.*)

33. INT. DAY. CITY PUB. 1978.

NILES, JOYCE *and* HARROP *sitting at a table looking at a menu.*
HARROP: Hot pot for me. Then jam roly-poly.
JOYCE: They do a damn fine steak-and-kidney in here,
    Wog. Extremely damn fine.
NILES: Sounds good.
JOYCE: Then I'm having . . . Yah, I'm going to sample the
    good old spotted dick. Christ, they've got bloody
    strawberry junket on here. Remember that stuff?
HARROP: Cow's afterbirth.
    (*Laughter.*)
NILES: I think I'll skip the dessert.

JOYCE: Yeah, as I was saying, there's this young guy—left school a couple of years ago. He's meant to be bloody quick. Playing for Sussex Colts at the moment.

HARROP: Sounds like rather serious good news, that. We've got to get him, Jerry. Get him opening the bowling with Wog here.

NILES (*preoccupied*): Sorry?

JOYCE (*glancing at* HARROP): Some young chap from school. Meant to be bloody quick.

NILES: Oh. Oh, great.

JOYCE (*seriously*): Funnily enough he reminded me of old Complex Colenso. Just his looks. Remember old Complex?

HARROP (*shaking head sadly*): Great shame. Bloody shame . . . still, life goes on and all that. (*Signals* WAITRESS) When you're ready, darling! (*Aside*) What is it, Tracy or Teresa?

JOYCE: Teresa.

(WAITRESS *approaches.*)

HARROP: Teresa, my lovely. We want one hot pot, two steak-and-kidneys. Got that, my sweet? Followed by one jam roly-poly and one spotted dick.

JOYCE (*false innocence*): Could I have an extra large spotted dick, Teresa?

(JOYCE *and* HARROP *suppress sniggers.*)

HARROP: Ignore this filthy old pervert, my darling girl. Now, another pint of wallop and a bouteille of château plonk. Red.

(WAITRESS *leaves.*)

JOYCE: Young commodity broker seeks meaningless physical relationship with well-endowed blond waitress.

(*Laughter.*)

HARROP: *Fabulous tits* . . . as Wordsworth said.

(*Great hilarity.*)

JOYCE: Did you see "Parkinson" last weekend? I thought it was one of his best shows.

34. INT. DAY. SCHOOL DINING ROOM. 1968.

The same meal, later on. Main course is being served up.
Establish MAID *in background, pushing a food trolley.*
JOYCE: A really hairy snatch is absolutely essential. (*A plate of stew is set in front of him. He looks down in horrified incredulity at his plate.*) Sweet bloody Jesus! Just what the hell is this supposed to be?
MOUNT: You're actually telling me that you would screw one of the maids, given the chance? Seriously?
JOYCE: Of course. I tell you when you're that desperate you don't care.
NILES: Come on, you must be bloody joking.
JOYCE: I'm not. Look, anyone would. It doesn't matter.
MOUNT: Any maid? You don't care which one?
JOYCE: Well, not every one, perhaps. I'd draw the line at that Spanish bint—the one with the split palate. (*Mimics speech defect*) Oh drarlee, kake me kake me. (*Laughter.*)

35. INT. DAY. CITY PUB. 1978.

Half an hour later. JOYCE *and* HARROP *noticeably more expansive.*
JOYCE: Just look at Alisdair Mount, for Christ's sake.
NILES: What about Alisdair?
JOYCE: Poor bastard. Married a moaner.
HARROP: God, you're not jesting. Poor bugger. Do you know her, Wog? Alisdair's wife?
NILES: Well, yes . . . Well, no, not really.
JOYCE: Hoo. Rather him than me. (*Makes an upward clawing motion.*) Boy, has she got him. Really got him.

(*Genuinely sad*) Poor old Alisdair. Come back from bloody Belfast—

HARROP: And moan bloody moan, all bloody day long. (*Imitating shrewish voice*) "Where do you think you're going? Oh God. Not playing cricket again. You and your bloody friends." I heard her once, gave him a right bollocking. Poor sod . . . Ah, your shout, Woggy, I believe.

JOYCE (*sadly*): Bloody women.

36. INT. DAY. SCHOOL DINING ROOM. 1968.

Same meal, toward the end.

JOYCE: I'm sorry, Wog, but you're wrong. There is absolutely no point in teaching sprogs like the junior colts moves like dummy scissors.

NILES: But they've got to learn sometime. The sooner the better, surely?

JOYCE (*patronizingly*): Too bloody complicated, my dear Wog. They couldn't find their arseholes with a mirror. (*Surreptitiously raises eyebrows at* MOUNT, *who acknowledges the look.*)

37. INT. DAY. CITY PUB. 1978.

JOYCE *and* HARROP *are halfway through their second bottle and on to cigars. Ties have been loosened.*

NILES *looks miserable. The other two are laughing.*

JOYCE (*making an effort to concentrate*): Sorry, Wog, sorry. You were saying.

NILES: About a job . . . You know, I was just wondering what the possibilities were. These days. If there . . .

JOYCE: Yah. (*Rubs chin.*) You're in personnel, aren't you?

NILES: Um, no. Sales, actually.

JOYCE: Ooh, Sales. Yah, mmmm . . . Look, tell you what

I'll do, Woggy. I'll keep the old ear firmly pinned to the ground and give you a buzz if I hear of anything. How's that? . . . Good Christ, look at the time!

38. EXT. NIGHT. A PARTICULARLY SEEDY BIT OF EARLS COURT. 1978.

NILES *scrutinizing the massed ranks of bell pushes in doorways. CU of one bearing the legend "J. COX."*

39. INT. NIGHT. COX'S STUDY. 1968.

CU COX *sitting at desk, apparently obsessed with the work in front of him. Camera pans around the study finding all its occupants similarly preoccupied. Then hold on* MOUNT, *standing motionless at door, a clipboard in his hand.* MOUNT *paces slowly around the room staring at the bowed heads.*

MOUNT: Haircut, Guthrie.

GUTHRIE: Oh *please*, Mount. Next week, *please*.

MOUNT: Bloody *haircut*, Guthrie! (*Pause.*) Haircut, Tregear. (*Writes names down. Stops at* COX'S *desk.* COX *manifestly does not need a haircut. The nape of his neck—which we see from* MOUNT'S *POV—is cruelly shorn.*) Haircut, Cox. (*Writes down name.*)

COX: I had a haircut last week, Mount.

MOUNT (*viciously*): Haircut, Animal.

COX: But, Mount—

(MOUNT, *with a sudden movement, pushes* COX'S *entire desk construction down onto the floor.*)

MOUNT: I said haircut, you little bastard. (*Nervous laughter from the others.* COX *surveys his ruined desk implacably.*)

40. INT. NIGHT. COX'S BEDSIT. 1978.

The bedsit is small and loathsome. A bed, a tiny sink unit, a Baby Belling cooker encrusted with grime, enamel-topped table

70

and assorted chairs. *Everywhere are stacks of accumulated*
possessions and unsteady piles of old newspapers and magazines.
On the wall are various leftist posters—Che, a peace dove, a
"Troops Out" broadsheet, etc.
The room is quite dark.
COX *and* NILES *stand in the middle of the room.* NILES *is clearly a*
little discountenanced.
COX *is at ease. His cynicism has an adamantine cast this evening.*
NILES: Jesus. Is this where you live?
COX: At the moment. It's only temporary. I find it
   useful . . . for my work. Sort of incognito, if you
   know what I mean.
NILES (*looking around*): Oh . . . (*uneasy laugh, notices posters*)
   What are you, Cox, some kind of red or something?
COX (*ignoring him*): Have a seat. Make yourself at home, as
   they say.
   (NILES *sits cautiously on the bed.*
   COX *puts a record on his Dansette. A tinny rendition of*
   "Badge" by Cream issues forth.)
NILES: Oh great. I love this. I've got it too. Play it all the
   time.
COX (*bitterly*): Takes you back, doesn't it?

41. INT. NIGHT. DORMITORY. 1968.

Sleeping dormitory.
Move in on COX's *bed. CU* COX's *face, expressionless, awake.*
COX *gets out of bed and moves silently through the beds toward*
the door.

42. INT. NIGHT. COX'S BEDSIT. 1978.

NILES *sitting at the small table.*
COX *puts a plate in front of him.*
NILES: What's this?

(*It's a hard-boiled egg, unhalved, with a blob of mayonnaise on the side.*)

COX: Egg mayonnaise. Don't worry, I haven't spat on it.

NILES: Sorry?

COX: Don't you remember? At school? How everyone used to spit in my food.

NILES (*embarrassed*): Christ. Surely not.

COX (*airily*): Oh yes. I must have sampled most people's saliva in my time. Yours, too, I shouldn't be surprised.

NILES: Jesus. Come off it.

COX: Well. Not to worry. That's all in the past, as they say. We've got a sardine salad to follow, and then a couple of yogurts. Simple fare (*unreal smile*) but the best. Cider?

43. INT. NIGHT. SCHOOL CORRIDOR. 1968.

COX *creeping along a dark and deserted corridor. Halts to listen.*

44. INT. NIGHT. COX'S BEDSIT. 1978.

After the meal.

NILES *is absent.*

COX *dumps a bulging concertina file on the table and sits down. A moment or two later* NILES *comes in, his face wrinkled with disgust.*

NILES: Jesus bloody Christ! That bog doesn't half stink.
(*Waves hands in front of face.*) God, how can you stand it? What the hell goes on in there anyway?
(*Suppresses a gag*) Christ. (*Sits down and breathes deeply.* COX *watches with an amused smile.* NILES *indicates the concertina file*) What's this?

72

COX: This? This is the Alisdair Mount file.

NILES (*groaning*): Oh no. Not a-bloody-gain. Bloody crap you talk.

COX: Call it what you like, but these are facts. The facts about Alisdair Mount.

NILES: What exactly is it you've got against Alisdair?

COX: What have I got against "Alisdair"? He's a soldier, isn't he? He goes to Northern Ireland, doesn't he?

NILES: So what? So do lots of other people.

COX: Oh yeah. But what's it like for someone like Alisdair Mount in Northern Ireland? What does Mount get up to? Never really thought about it, have you? What it's like for Mount in Northern Ireland. I'll tell you what it's like. It's a bloody paradise. (*Taps file*) It's all in there.

NILES: I see. I see.

(*Sits back.*) So what does Alisdair do then?

COX: What do you think he does? You say he's your friend. What do you think he does?

NILES: Me? Christ, I don't bloody know. You're the one making the bloody accusations. You tell me, mate.

COX: Do you want to know?

NILES: Yeah. God, we've got this far.

COX: I'll tell you what Alisdair Mount does.

NILES: Go on then.

COX: He buggers people up.

(*Pause.*

NILES *can't think of anything to say.* COX *seems lost in thought.*)

45. INT. NIGHT. BOOT ROOM STAIRS 1968.

COX *creeping down boot room stairs. Absolute silence.*

46. INT. NIGHT. COX'S BEDSIT. 1978.

NILES *and* COX *sitting at the table, the file between them.*
NILES *is looking around, shaking his head slightly in the manner
of someone who can't believe what he's just heard. He is angry,
but has decided to humor* COX—*something which, in the
following exchange, he makes a bad job of.*
NILES: Jesus. (*Shakes head.*)
You realize . . . you realize just exactly what it is
you're asking me to do, don't you?
COX: It's not much. Just some information.
NILES: Not much? Spy on . . . Inform. . . ? Not much?
(*False laugh.*) Jesus Christ, you're bloody priceless, you
are. God . . . He's my *friend*, you . . . you great
bloody tit. Don't you realize that? Don't you know
what it means?
COX: He's not your friend. Any more than those other
cretins you play cricket with every weekend are.
Don't make me bloody laugh.
NILES (*shaking his head in wonder at this astonishing nonsense*):
What? Now I know it. (*Points finger at* COX) You're
bloody out of your tiny chinese, mate.
COX (*coolly*): He's not your friend. You're stupid enough to
think he is, but he's not. Neither are any of the others.
NILES: Oh no?
COX: Absolutely not.
NILES (*trying to control himself*): Then why do I see them all
the time? Tell me that, wise-arse. Why did I have
lunch today with Jerry Joyce and Mungo Harrop? Eh?
You see, you don't know what you're bloody talking
about, pal. I mean . . . (*shrugs*) Jesus, there's no big
deal . . . We were all powers together, for Christ's
sake. Powers. We play cricket for the Wanderers.
That's all. We're old school friends. *Old—school—
friends*. Full stop.

COX: You were a power for the same reason you play in the Wanderers. For the same reason you see them every week. For the same reason you claim they're your friends.

NILES: Oh yeah? And what's that?

COX (*anger breaking through the cynicism for a moment*): Because you can bowl a bloody googly, that's what! Convert a fucking try from the halfway line, that's what! Serve a bloody ace at tennis, that's bloody what! That's why, you dense bloody git. It's got absolutely bugger all—*bugger all*—to do with you!

NILES (*furiously*): Shut up! Shut bloody up! (*Gets to his feet.*) What are you talking about? What are you bloody talking about? Bloody Cox. Bloody Animal. (*Snatches jacket.*) I must be going mad myself to come here. Thanks for dinner. You can stuff your bloody dinner . . . (*gives him a savage V-sign*) up your tight communist arse . . .

COX (*patiently*): For God's sake—

NILES (*pointing at him*): I know what *you've* got against Alisdair Mount. And it's got nothing to do with Northern bloody Ireland! I'm getting out of here. (*Looks around*) Bloody cesspit. Bloody sewer.

COX: Look, calm down—

NILES: Don't you calm down me, Cox. I could eradicate you, Cox. Come down on you like a ton of hot bricks . . .
(*At door, disgustedly, bitterly*) It's people like you, Cox, wankers like you, that just . . . you just spoil everything. Anything you come near. You just . . . everything gets ruined. (*Slams door shut.*)
(*CU* COX *shaking head sadly, a little smile of satisfaction on his face.*)

47. INT. NIGHT. BOOT ROOM. 1968.

COX *settling down in a dark alcove. Lights a cigarette. Inhales deeply. CU of his contented face.*

48. EXT. DAY. CRICKET PITCH. 1978.

NILES *throwing down bat and gloves disgustedly. Sighs, looks up to sky, clenches fists, bares teeth in a silent growl of anger. Unknown to him all this is observed by* FRANCES, *sitting in a deck chair out of his sight. She looks curiously at him over her paperback copy of* Anna Karenina.

NILES *goes on admonishing himself, muttering, kicking bat, etc.*

FRANCES: Hello.

NILES: Oh. Um. Hello.

FRANCES: Something wrong?

NILES: What? Oh no. No, no. Nothing.

FRANCES: Didn't look like it, if you don't mind me saying so.

NILES: Nothing really. Just a bit of a cock-up on the field.

FRANCES: How many runs did you get?

NILES: Two.

FRANCES: And that's bad, is it?

NILES: Well, yes . . . Especially for me.

FRANCES: I see. (*Pause.*) Do you mind if I ask you a question?

NILES: No, not at all. Ask away.

FRANCES: Why do people call you "Wog"?

NILES (*uneasy laugh*): Oh, it was just my nickname at school.

FRANCES: Yes, I gathered that. But why that particular nickname?

NILES: I lived in Singapore, you see. My parents lived out there.

FRANCES: I'm afraid I still don't follow.

76

NILES: No . . . well, anyone who lived abroad was called "Wog." Anywhere abroad. For some reason you were automatically known as "Wog." Or, um, if you were, ah, very hairy.

FRANCES: What?

NILES: You were called "Wog" too. If you were . . . If you had a lot of body hair. Silly, really.

FRANCES: And you don't mind?

NILES: Mind what?

FRANCES: You don't mind still being called "Wog"? You don't mind being introduced to people—perfect strangers—as "Wog"?

NILES: Well . . . I don't really think about it.

FRANCES: You don't find it in any way . . . offensive?

NILES (*edgy laugh*): Um, no. Should I? I've never given it any thought. We all call each other by our nicknames. Just a habit. Jerry Joyce was called "Bog Door," for example.

FRANCES: What?

NILES: *Bog Door.* "Bog Door" Joyce, we used to call him.

FRANCES: Good Lord. Why?

NILES (*knowing laugh*): Oh, it's a long story . . . Actually, to tell you the truth, Jerry does object if you call him "Bog Door" these days. Ah well. What the hell, you know . . .

FRANCES: What is your name?

NILES: What, you mean my Christian name?

FRANCES: Yes. I'm afraid I can't bring myself to call you "Wog." Or "Woggy."

NILES: Oh. Right. It's, ah, Quentin. Quentin Niles.

FRANCES: Good. Quentin. (*Takes out cigarette.*) Have a cigarette, Quentin.

NILES: No thanks. I don't smoke. Ha-ha, only two out of three, ha-ha.

FRANCES: What?

NILES: Um, vices. Two out of, um, three.

FRANCES (*rummaging in hand bag*): Oh.

NILES (*deeply embarrassed*): Ha. (*Looks at scoreboard.*) Well.
(*Fake breeziness*) Old Alisdair seems to be going
along OK.

FRANCES: Oh, Alisdair will do all right, I daresay. Loves his
cricket, does Alisdair. (*Looks at* NILES) He says you are
a "Born Sportsman."

NILES: Does he? That's very kind of him.

FRANCES: What do you do? I mean, what's your job?

NILES: Me? I'm . . . in the motor trade.

FRANCES: That sounds rather grand. Are you terribly
successful in the motor trade?

NILES: Well . . .

FRANCES: Let me put it this way. With what aspect of the
motor trade do you concern yourself?

NILES: I'm the assistant regional sales manager for a small
automotive components firm.

FRANCES: Ah.

NILES: You know, we make shock absorbers, air filters,
that sort of thing. (FRANCES, *nodding, lights cigarette.*)
It's quite an interesting line, actually. Quite a
challenge in a way. It's a competitive market, you see.
But we're expanding, slowly but surely.

FRANCES: Fascinating.

NILES: I'm responsible for the Croydon area down to the
South coast.

FRANCES: Uh-huh.
(*Pause.*)

FRANCES: Where do you live?

NILES: Notting Hill. Well, sort of.

FRANCES: You're terribly vague about yourself.

NILES: Am I?

FRANCES: Yes. "Motor trade." "Notting Hill sort of."

NILES: Sorry, I—

FRANCES: Where exactly in Notting Hill? Which street?
(*Level gaze. Cut as if to* NILES, *but instead cut to Scene 49.*)

49. INT. NIGHT. SCHOOL DINING ROOM. 1968.

CU: NILES's *vacant sweaty face.*
Pull back to reveal dining room cleared for the school dance. A makeshift disco, a few streamers, pop posters. An amoebic light show is projected on one wall and there is the intermittent flashing of a strobe light.
The music—loud—is "Strange Brew" by Cream.
NILES *is dancing with studied psychedelic élan. A girl jogs non-committally in front of him.*
Other couples occupy the dance floor.
At one end of the room a group of boys whisper to each other and stare at the unclaimed girls.
A buffet dinner of sorts has been laid out and there is a soft-drinks bar tended by MOUNT *and* JOYCE.
Shadowy figures of staff chaperones can be made out on a dais at the far end. The boys are in "civilian" clothes, aiming at trendiness but, with the exception of JOYCE *who wears a white suit from Lord John, falling well short: a velvet jacket here, a string of beads there, the odd satin shirt, flares, huge buckled belts on pale hipster trousers.*
NILES, *in similar pursuit of modishness, has parted his hair in the middle and wears a small Indian silk scarf at his neck secured with a silver woggle. He is also wearing desert boots, otherwise his sports jacket and trousers are unexceptionally normal.*
The music ends.
NILES's *dance-floor cool instantly deserts him.*
NILES: Would you like something to eat?
GIRL (*strong regional accent*): Yes. OK.
(*They go to the buffet table. Large trays of chicken in a*

79

cream sauce, bowls of sweet-corn and baked potatoes. They
serve themselves.)
NILES (*hopelessly formal*): Are you doing "A" levels?
GIRL: Yeah. Maths, Physics and Chemistry. What about you?
NILES: I'm doing "S" level actually.
GIRL: What's that?
NILES (*ignoring her*): English, Biology and Geography.
GIRL: That's an odd mixture.
NILES: What board are you doing?
GIRL: What do you mean, "what board"?
NILES: The people who set the paper. Is it London or . . .
  or Oxford and Cambridge?
GIRL: I don't know. Is it important?
NILES (*fainty desperate*): I'm doing Oxford and Cambridge. I
  shall probably be going to Oxford. Or Cambridge.
GIRL: Oh.
NILES: Would you like a baked potato?
  (*He leans forward to prong one with his fork and as he does
  so a corner of his jacket trails in the chicken and cream
  sauce.*
  NILES *doesn't notice this. He resumes his nervous prattle.*)
  Of course I don't know yet what I will be reading at
  Oxford or Cambridge. Probably English I should think,
  though everyone says PPE's a soft option and I—
GIRL: Excuse me, but you've got chicken all over your
  jacket and trousers.
NILES: God! Shit! Oh Christ, sorry. (*He maniacally starts to
  wipe it clean.*) Jesus. Hang on, let me get you a drink.
  Orange juice or fruit punch? They won't allow Coca-
  Cola, I'm sorry to say.
GIRL: Orange juice, please. Are you sure your jacket's OK?
NILES: Oh yes, of course. Um, do you want your orange
  juice a bit—you know?
GIRL: Sorry?

NILES: With a bit more—you know—*zap.*

GIRL: I'm sorry. I just don't know what you're talking about.

NILES: Never mind. Leave it to me.
(*Wags finger and delivers what he takes to be a knowing smile.*) Don't go away now.
(*He scurries over to the bar.*
JOYCE, MOUNT, COLENSO *and* HARROP *cluster around. There's an air of excited conspiracy.*
Falsetto) Two orange juices, please, mister.
(*Basso profundo*)
And spike'em good.

MOUNT: What's she like, Woggy?

NILES: Proper yobess. *And* doing Maths, Physics and Chemistry. Just my bloody luck, I ask you.

HARROP: Christ. At least she's got decent tits. (*Pours drinks.*) In fact she's got extremely bloody decent tits. Any chance?

NILES: Haven't the faintest. She seems bored stiff. I thought you said they were sex-starved. As sex-starved as us, you said.

COLENSO: They've all got oik boyfriends. I told you.

JOYCE: What are they bloody doing here then?

MOUNT: Is she incredibly "ee by goom"?

NILES: Well . . . yeah, I suppose so. But why don't you guys dance? Why aren't you guys dancing?

JOYCE (*offended*): Get knotted, Wog. Have you seen what the bloody slags look like? Wouldn't touch them with a barge pole.

COLENSO (*Deep South accent*): Why, what you doin' wit dat ting, Rastus? (*Sniggers and suppressed laughs from the others.* JOYCE *takes the glasses of orange juice below the level of the bar where he adds slugs of gin.*)

MOUNT: They say some old bat will be going around

81

during the slow dances. To make sure everyone's twelve inches apart. With a bloody ruler.

HARROP: Bloody marvelous.

MOUNT: Frigging waste of time if you ask me.

NILES: Slam a lot of that stuff in, will you, Bog Door?

JOYCE: Relax, Woggy, will you?

MOUNT: Save it. I think we should bugger off back to the house.

NILES: Now? Hang about. I think she was getting quite pash. I've got a chance of a decent snog here.

MOUNT: I think we should get out of here, with the booze, get back to the house and get pissed out of our minds.

JOYCE: Bloody right.

COLENSO: Too bloody right.

NILES: Give us a minute or two.

(*Turns around with drinks.*) Oh, *Christ.* Where the hell's she got to now?

50. EXT. DAY. STREET OUTSIDE NILES'S FLAT. 1978.

NILES *walking angrily down the street dogged by* COX.

COX *catches up with him.*

NILES (*angry whisper*): Look. Just piss off, will you? Just piss bloody off.

COX: Listen. About the other night, no hard feelings, OK?

NILES (*astonished*): What?

COX: No hard feelings. It was . . . you were a bit worked up. A bit uptight.

NILES: *Me?*

COX: OK, OK. *Me.* I'm sorry. It's this job I'm doing. It has its pressures, you know. I don't think you realize. It's difficult. There are all kinds of pressures.

NILES (*to himself*): Jesus Christ Almighty.

COX: Look. About Alisdair Mount—

NILES: Just keep Alisdair Mount out of it. I told you. I'm

not going to do a bloody thing. Not a bloody thing,
got it? (*Pause.*) I just don't understand you, Cox.
People like you. Alisdair . . . Christ, Alisdair's just
got a bloody job to do, like anyone else. That's all
there is to it. Leave it alone, for God's sake. That's the
best bit of advice you're ever going to get. (*Pause.*)
What have you got against him, anyway? What's so
special about Alisdair?
(COX *says nothing. He just looks at* NILES
incredulously) Oh no. Surely not . . . Jesus Christ,
Cox. Not after all these years. Not the boot room.
Don't tell me it's the bloody boot room.

51. INT. NIGHT. THE BOOT ROOM. 1968

CU COX *smoking in the boot room, snug in his alcove. There is
absolutely no sound.*

52. EXT. NIGHT. SCHOOL GROUNDS. 1968.

Noisy bustling group of MOUNT, JOYCE, NILES, HARROP,
COLENSO *and two or three others striding powerfully and
impatiently along, passing around and swigging from half-bottles
of gin.*
MOUNT (*elated*): Slags! Bloody vile slags!
HARROP: Well . . . There were one or two.
JOYCE: God, they were revolting.
COLENSO: God, they were foul.
MOUNT: Jesus. Foul bloody tarts.
COLENSO: Christ, did you see that one? The one with the
bloody enormous fat legs. Bloody grotesque!
(*Laughter and general mirth from the others at this
recollection.*)

53. INT. NIGHT. THE BOOT ROOM. 1968.

COX, *in the same position as Scene 51. Still absolutely no noise.*
COX *slowly sits forward, cocks his head to one side as though
listening for some faint sound.*

54. EXT. DAY. BEHIND CRICKET PAVILION. 1978.

NILES, *in whites, sitting alone behind the pavilion. His head is
canted in exactly the same manner as* COX's. *He stands up and
walks slowly and cautiously around the side of the pavilion.
We can hear indistinct voices.*
NILES *edges forward.*
Camera tracks around the corner to discover MOUNT *and* HARROP
sitting in deck chairs, unaware that they are being overheard.
MOUNT: Good Lord. When was this exactly?
HARROP: Not long ago. A week or so back.
MOUNT: And he came to see you? For a job?
HARROP: Not me, exactly. It was Jerry he wanted to see.
MOUNT: Oh. What were you doing there?
HARROP: Jerry asked me along. Moral support, you know.
MOUNT: God, yeah. Fairly necessary, I'd have thought . . .
    Good God. And he actually wanted a job? Wanted
    Jerry to get him a job?
HARROP: Well, yes. I think that was the general idea.
MOUNT: In the City? Can you see him in the City? Really.
HARROP: I think that was what he was hoping for.
    (*Chuckles.*) He seemed quite desperate, actually. Rather
    down in the mouth.
MOUNT: Bit of a cheek though, all the same. Bit of a nerve,
    don't you think? I mean, Jesus, really . . . What on
    earth did he expect Jerry to do?
HARROP: God knows. Pull some strings or something.
MOUNT: What did Jerry say, for Christ's sake?
HARROP: The usual stuff. Ear to the ground, see what he
    could do. That kind of routine.

MOUNT: And did that satisfy him?

HARROP: Oh yeah. Sort of pathetically grateful, if you know what I mean.

MOUNT: God. (*Chuckles.*) Poor bloody sod, eh?

HARROP (*laughs*): Same old story. Poor old Wog, desperately tagging on for all he's worth.

(*Cut to* NILES.

Fade out MOUNT's *words.*

CU NILES, *face set.*)

55. EXT. NIGHT. SCHOOL GROUNDS. 1968.

Same group as Scene 52, striding along through the night with the same brisk, booze-inspired purpose.

MOUNT: God, oh God, they were foul. Dis-gusting. Re-volting.

JOYCE: Enough to turn you into a rabid homo.

COLENSO: Oh yeah?

(*General laughter.*)

JOYCE: Shag off, Colenso.

MOUNT: Thank Christ I'm getting pissed. Swig, Wog?

NILES: Great. (*Drinks.*) Wow! Jesus, am I going to get totally zonked. (*Takes a long pull on the bottle.*)

MOUNT (*punching* COLENSO): Christ, look at old Woggy there! Look at Wog go!

(*General laughter and horseplay. A sense of a sodality having formed.*)

56. INT. DAY. NILES'S FLAT. 1978.

NILES *sitting disconsolately at the typewriter. Noise of reggae coming from below stairs.*

NILES *massages his temples.*

CU typewriter.

We read: "Dear Jerry, many thanks for lunch last week. I was

wondering if any news had come your way. Sorry to be so
impatient! The problem is that—"
NILES *removes paper from the typewriter. Reads it. Then he spits*
on it, crumples it into a ball and throws it away. Sits for a
moment, head in hands. There's a knock on the door.
NILES *gets up and opens it.* FRANCES *stands there.*
FRANCES (*quite relaxed*): Hello. I was passing. I thought I'd
   look in.
NILES (*trying to conceal his panic*): Oh, hello. Christ . . . Nice
   to see you. Look, come in. Come in.
(FRANCES *saunters in and looks idly around. Behind her,* NILES
   desperately scrutinizes the untidy room, but realizes there's
   nothing he can do.) Sorry about the mess.
FRANCES: What on earth is that noise?
NILES: You mean from downstairs? It's the people in the flat
   below. They're Rastafarians, you see.
FRANCES: Bit loud all the same, isn't it?
NILES: Oh, I don't really mind. Get used to it after a while.
FRANCES: I wouldn't stand for it, I can tell you.
   (FRANCES *goes to the window and looks out on the street.*
   NILES *spots a* Penthouse *magazine on a chair and throws a*
   newspaper over it.) Nice view.
NILES: Sorry?
FRANCES: The view. Very nice.
NILES: Oh. Oh yes. (*Pause*) Were, um, you out shopping?
FRANCES: Yes. Sort of. (*Laughs*) God, I'm beginning to
   sound like you. (*She picks up* NILES'*s team photo*) Good
   Lord. Is that Alisdair? So it is. Look, there's you.
NILES: Yes. (*Nervous laugh*) Great team, we were. Unbeaten.
   Would you like some coffee?
FRANCES (*lighting a cigarette*): Please. (*She stoops to pick up the*
   crumpled ball of paper) Is this important?
NILES: Oh, no. Just trying to write a letter. Job hunting.
   (*Looks thoughtful.*)
FRANCES: Tiring of the motor trade?

NILES: What?

FRANCES: Are you tiring of the motor trade? You made it sound quite exciting the last time we spoke.

(*She picks up the newspaper and spots the magazine. She picks it up*) Gracious. Do you still read this stuff? (*She flicks through it*) Alisdair buys them too, you know. I keep coming across his hiding places. He keeps them stashed away. Little stores of them. Like a squirrel.

NILES (*covered in confusion*): Actually it's not mine. In fact.

FRANCES: You never really change, do you?

NILES: Who? Me?

FRANCES: You lot (*pause*) . . . never *really* change.

NILES: I don't get you. I'm afraid I don't understand.

FRANCES: Never mind. Not important.

NILES: Another chap left it here actually. A guy I knew at school. He came around, you see.

FRANCES: From school? You mean to say he just happened to have this with him? Rather proves my point, don't you think?

NILES (*a little desperately*): Actually he was interested in Alisdair.

FRANCES: Alisdair? What on earth for?

NILES: He said he was a journalist, an investigative journalist. He asked me if I knew anything about Alisdair's job.

FRANCES: In the army?

NILES: In Northern Ireland. If it was important. Secret, dangerous, that sort of thing. What sort of thing Alisdair got up to.

FRANCES: How strange. They warn him about journalists, you know. Warn them all about talking. But I've no idea what Alisdair does. He never talks about it, not even to me.

NILES: Yes, that's more or less what I said. To this chap. More or less told him to clear off too.

FRANCES (*vaguely*): He does have a gun though. A pistol thing. So I suppose it must be dangerous.

NILES: Alisdair? What? You mean he sort of always has a gun on him? Over here?

FRANCES: Yes. Well, not *on* him exactly. He keeps it in the car. I won't have it in the house.

NILES: But why?

FRANCES: I just don't like guns.

NILES: No. I mean, why does he have a gun?

FRANCES: I don't know. You know what Alisdair's like. He likes shooting it, I suppose . . . Something about the IRA, he says. He says you can't be too careful. People seem to be targets these days. But he's always had guns around him, Alisdair. As long as I've known him anyway. Loves shooting. Shoot anything, will Alisdair. (*Ironically*) "Happiness is a warm gun." I used to say that should be our theme song.

NILES: Ah.

(*During her last speech* FRANCES *has moved slightly closer to* NILES. *She stands looking at him, fairly close to him. Her manner is wholly at ease: the invitation is silently proffered; it's there for* NILES *to accept if he feels inclined.*

NILES *makes no move.*)

FRANCES (*sardonically*): Here's your mag.

NILES (*taking it*): I'll chuck it away.

(NILES *gladly moves away from* FRANCES. *Throws the magazine in a wastepaper basket.*

FRANCES *stubs out her cigarette angrily.*)

FRANCES: Well, I'd better be off. Leave you to your magazine.

NILES: Look, I told you—

FRANCES: Sorry, that wasn't fair. Sorry. (*She looks at him.*) You're uncomfortable, aren't you? Just incredibly . . . uncomfortable?

NILES: Me? God, of course not.

FRANCES: Exactly like Alisdair. Well, in some ways.

NILES: Am I? How?

FRANCES: It must really kink you up when you're locked away in those places. Does it? Kink you up like that?

NILES: I'm sorry. I just don't know what you mean.

FRANCES (*false breeziness*): Never mind, never mind . . . Well, lovely to have seen you, Quentin. I must run along.

(NILES *goes to the door and holds it open for her. Then he suddenly becomes aware of the opportunity he's just missed.*)

NILES: It was nice . . . I'm very glad you came by, I mean do . . . I mean just drop in—if you're passing, that is. I'm sorry, um, I was a bit on edge today. It's this job business.

FRANCES: I should have phoned, I suppose.

(*Pause.*

NILES *almost writhes with embarrassment and awkwardness.*)

NILES: No, please don't bother . . . to phone. I mean you don't need to check—God, that sounds terrible. What I mean is I'd be very glad . . . very happy to see you any time. (*Pause.*) I'd like to think that you could come by whenever you felt like it. If, that is, you want to. (*Hold on* NILES's *agonized face. The dull sound of reggae from down below suddenly stops.*)

57. INT. NIGHT. THE BOOT ROOM. 1968.

NILES, MOUNT, HARROP, COLENSO et al., *silently, menacingly descending the darkened stairs of the boot room.*
There's the sound of a door being closed firmly.
Suddenly the place is bathed in harsh light as a switch is turned.
COX *is discovered, blinking blindly, huddling in his alcove.*
Cut to MOUNT. *CU his bullish, flushed face.*

MOUNT: Well, well, well. Look what we've got here.

58. INT. DAY. NILES'S OFFICE. 1978.

COX *and* NILES *stand facing each other.*
COX *is almost unnaturally at ease but looks very decrepit and seedy.*
NILES *is uncomfortable, edgy and irritated.*

COX: Do you know what I remember best? I remember that I couldn't even have a shit in peace. You've no idea what a luxury it was to go home in the holidays and have a crap—uninterrupted, unobserved. (*Slight laugh*) Undisturbed by prying eyes. Have you *any* idea what that was like, Niles? Have you got any idea? . . . No, of course you bloody haven't. Not a bloody clue. (*Pause.*) Even the first-year skunks hated me.

NILES: Oh, come *on*.

COX: No, they did. Everybody did. It was a way of getting in, of showing how—

NILES: Look, can't you give it a rest? It's all over now. In the past. Water under the bridge. Forget it.

COX: Ah, but that's just it, you see.

NILES: What?

COX: I can't. Or rather, I don't want to.

NILES: Don't want to what?

COX: Forget it.

NILES: Well, that's your business.
(*Pause.*)

COX: Funny thing about revenge . . .

NILES: What do you mean?

COX (*as if to himself*): How it lives on with you. You'd expect it to die away, wouldn't you? With time. But no. It doesn't. It gets stronger. But, one thing does change. Revenge itself isn't enough. Not on its own. Not just any old revenge. It's got to be right. The right sort. What you might call "apt." Know what I mean?

NILES (*testily*): No.

COX (*thoughtfully*): Apt.

NILES: Give it a rest, will you? For God's sake.

COX (*thoughtfully*): No friends. No friends at all. No one likes you. Know what that's like?

NILES: Jesus. What do you want me to do? Cry?

COX: No. I just want you to help me out.

NILES: Good God, don't start on that again. Why me, for Christ's sake? Why pick on me? Out of the whole bloody school you pick on me.

COX: Exactly.

NILES: What do you mean?

COX: Because we've got something in common.

NILES (*incredulous*): You *must* be kidding.

COX: You and I, we're . . . how shall I put it? We're on the outside, if you see what I'm getting at. Solitaries. We are . . . not part of the group.

NILES: What do you mean, group? What are you talking about?

COX: What group are you in, then?

(*CU* NILES *as this sinks in. Pause.*)

NILES (*dully*): Look, just piss off and leave me alone, will you? You bloody shag. Just . . . forget it. What do you know?

COX (*intensely*): Just tell me anything you can about him. Anything you can. Any information. You don't owe him anything. Any little thing you can tell me. Anything you can think of. Anything you've found out.

(NILES *keeps his gaze fixed on the wall.*)

NILES: It's no good. He doesn't talk about the army. His wife told me. He never mentions it. (*He realizes the implications of what he's just said.*) It just came up in casual conversation.

COX: I see . . . Well, anything you can remember. It might

not seem important to you.

(NILES *pauses: it's a crucial moment.*)

NILES: He has a gun. He keeps it in his car. (*Looks up to meet* COX's *gaze*) That's all I know. That's all I can tell you.

59. INT. NIGHT. MOUNT'S HOUSE. 1978.

A plush, rather staid living room.

FRANCES *sitting in an armchair, silent.*

MOUNT *playing with a labrador on the hearth rug.* FRANCES *stares at him as he fusses over and teases the dog.*

FRANCES: I went to your friend's flat the other day. Saturday.

MOUNT: My friend?

FRANCES: Yes. "Fog." "Dog," or whatever.

MOUNT: Mmm?

FRANCES: The one who's good at games.

MOUNT: Oh, *Wog.* You mean Woggy Niles.

FRANCES: That's the one.

MOUNT (*vaguely curious*): What on earth made you go and see Wog Niles, for God's sake?

FRANCES: I told you I bumped into him the other day. Didn't I tell you?

MOUNT: No, you didn't, actually.

FRANCES: Didn't I? Well, I bumped into him while I was shopping and he asked me for tea.

MOUNT (*shaking head in wonder*): Good Lord. Wonders will never cease. Must be cracking up, old Wog.

FRANCES: And what's that supposed to mean?

MOUNT (*ignoring her*): You know, Mungo Harrop told me Wog was after a job. In the City.

FRANCES: What's so strange about that?

MOUNT: Can you see Wog in the City? Wog, in the City? Extraordinary chap.

(*Pause.*)

FRANCES: Is he any good at tennis?

MOUNT: Wog? Yes, bloody good as far as I can remember.

FRANCES: Do you think you could persuade him to come around here and give me a few lessons?

MOUNT: Yes. Sure. I'll ask him on Saturday. Wog'll be delighted.

(*Returning to the dog and speaking to it as if to a child*) Won't he, boy? Won't he, boy? Wog'll be delighted, won't he?

(*CU* FRANCES *looking at him.*

Cut as if back to MOUNT *on the rug, but instead cut to Scene 60.*)

60. INT. NIGHT. THE BOOT ROOM 1968.

MOUNT *advancing confidently on the cowering* COX.

CU COX*'s shocked face.*

Cut, as if back to MOUNT, *instead come in on next scene.*

61. INT. DAY. BEDROOM IN MOUNT'S HOUSE. 1978.

Extreme CU of NILES*'s troubled face. He takes his bottom lip between his teeth. Shuts his eyes. He is trembling very slightly. Slowly pull back to reveal the bedroom and* FRANCES *lying in bed behind* NILES.

FRANCES *is relaxed, mildly amused.*

NILES *is in tennis gear, he has only removed his shirt.*

NILES: I feel such an almighty bloody shit.

FRANCES: I'd save the torment till later. You've not actually got around to doing anything yet.

NILES: But it's just that I feel that . . . Well, Alisdair *is* my oldest friend.

FRANCES: Oh, for God's sake.

NILES (*miserably*): You don't know what it's like. It's a terrible betrayal. A betrayal of trust.

93

FRANCES: I wouldn't fret too much on that score.

NILES (*tensing, suspicious*): What do you mean by that?

FRANCES (*sighing*): Perhaps you ought to know that . . . (*she pauses, thinks better of this explanation*) Look, why don't you let me do the worrying, OK?

NILES (*head in hands*): Oh, God. God.

FRANCES (*lights a cigarette*): This is absurd. We'll forget all about it if you like.

NILES: But you see . . . what I can't take is if he ever found out.

FRANCES: He won't find out.

NILES: Why not?

FRANCES (*deliberately*): Because Alisdair is very, *very* stupid.

NILES: *Alisdair?* Surely—

FRANCES: He is. He's as stupid as . . . as—(*Shrugs.*)

NILES (*taking this in*): My God.

(*Pause.*

NILES *seems to be wrestling with some concept.*)

I was trying to work something out the other day. I was thinking about us. Well, about myself. I thought: if you've led a public life for ten years, if everything you do—washing, eating, sleeping, everything—is done in the company of other people for ten years. If there are no secrets . . . no solitude. Then, if that's the case, if that's the world you've grown up in, then it's going to be extremely hard to learn how to be private again when you leave. Extremely hard to get a private life going.

(FRANCES *moves down the bed. She presses herself against* NILES*'s back.*)

You see, when you're there, it's twenty-four hours a day. A completely public life, shared with everyone. Everybody knows everything about you. You can't hide anything.

(FRANCES *rests her chin on his shoulder.*

94

He stands up and moves to the window. He parts the
curtains an inch or two and looks out.)

62. EXT. DAY. LANE OUTSIDE MOUNT'S HOUSE. 1978.

NILES's *POV: A flash of white in the trees and bushes opposite*
the house.

63. INT. DAY. MOUNT'S BEDROOM. 1978.

CU NILES's *face staring out.*
Hold for a couple of seconds.
Then NILES *turns and looks back at the bed and* FRANCES.
Cut immediately to Scene 64.

64. INT. NIGHT. THE BOOT ROOM. 1968.

CU COX's *face in a rictus of agony, pressed against the boot*
room floor. MOUNT *sits on his back holding* COX's *arms in a*
double nelson. The others look on casually, enjoying themselves.
MOUNT: You've had it, you little bastard. Bloody had it.
    We've got punishments for bloody smokers, Cox.
    Serious crime, smoking is, Cox. (*Leans forward and*
    whispers evilly in COX's *ear.*) Special category of
    punishments for wankers like you, Cox.
JOYCE: Toothpaste up his arse.
COLENSO: Blackball him.
JOYCE: Let's give him the toothpaste. A whole tonking
    tube.
HARROP: Let's do both.
    (*General laughter and agreement. The mood is not feverish,*
    simply confident, matter-of-fact and quite good fun.)
MOUNT: I've got a better idea. Let's shave his pubes off.
    (*Shouts of acclaim greet his idea.*)
COLENSO: Get his bloody pajama trousers off.

95

MOUNT: Get a razor, someone.

(JOYCE *leaves.*

MOUNT *puts his mouth to* COX's *ear.*) We're going to shave your pubes off, Cox. Got that? That's the punishment. Removal of pubic hair.

HARROP: If he's got any.

(*Laughter.*)

COLENSO: Right, let's see.

(COX's *pajama trousers are wrenched down, removed and thrown away.* MOUNT *turns him over.*

COX *begins to struggle and fight. The others gather and hold him down. There are no sadistic or maniacal expressions. The mood is still one of loutish fun, drunken horseplay.*

COX *panics and starts to scream. He is swiftly gagged with his pajama bottoms.*

COLENSO *flourishes boot polish and a brush before* COX's *rolling, boggling eyes.*) Nice black dubbin, Animal.

(JOYCE *returns with a razor and a can of shaving foam.*)

JOYCE: Got it.

HARROP: All quiet?

JOYCE: Not a sound.

MOUNT: You can forget about the bloody foam. Just give me the razor. Right, Cox . . .

(COX *squirms and kicks out in desperation and manages to free one leg.*)

Get his sodding leg, Woggy!

(COX's *furiously kicking leg connects with* HARROP.)

HARROP: Ouch! You little shag! (*He punches* COX *in the ribs.*)

MOUNT: Get that frigging leg, Wog!

(NILES *moves forward and grabs* COX's *leg.*)

HARROP: What shall we do? Dubbin him first or shave him first?

(*Laughter: even at this moment there are no second thoughts.*)

MOUNT: Shave him. (*To* cox) Keep very still, Cox. Can you hear me? You'd better listen, arsehole, or you could have a very nasty accident. Something you might find you'll regret for the rest of your life. (*He looks around at the laughing faces. Only* NILES *looks vaguely troubled.*)
So keep very still, Cox. Very still. I should hate my hand to slip.
(*He bends to his task.*
CU cox's *horror-struck face. Amplified sound of razor rasp.*
cox *screams through his gag. Cut to Scene 65.*)

65. INT. DAY. MOUNT'S VOLVO. 1978.

MOUNT *driving.* NILES *sitting beside him in the front in sports clothes, sweaty and somewhat disheveled and holding a tennis racket.*
They are driving along a leafy un-built-up stretch of suburban road that leads away from MOUNT'S *house.*
MOUNT: I can't believe that was the first time you'd been out to the house
NILES: Yes, it was, actually. Funnily enough.
MOUNT: Good Lord. I could have sworn we had you out for a meal. Didn't you come and eat once?
NILES: No. I don't think so. I mean, I'm sure I haven't.
MOUNT: Good God. Thanks anyway for the coaching, Wog. How was the old girl?
NILES: She was quite good, actually. Really quite good.
(NILES *looks out of the window.*
From NILES's *POV we suddenly see a flash of white in the greenery beside the road.* NILES *whirls around, but sees nothing more.*)
MOUNT: What is it?
NILES: I thought I saw someone. Must be mistaken.

97

MOUNT: Oh.

> (*Pause.*)

NILES: Frances said you had a gun.

MOUNT: Help yourself.

> (MOUNT *leans forward and opens the glove compartment. Reticently,* NILES *takes out an old Colt revolver. He weighs it in his hand.*)

NILES: Jesus Christ. It's much heavier than you'd expect.

MOUNT (*odd smile*): It was my father's. It's licensed and everything. I just like to have it around. You can't be too careful these days, you know, Wog. (NILES *puts the gun back.*)

NILES: IRA?

MOUNT: Savage bastards, Woggy, savage bastards. You can't be too careful.

NILES: I suppose not. (*Pause.*) Do you remember a guy called Cox? Guy at school?

MOUNT (*looks around*): Cox? . . . No. I don't think so. Was he in our house?

66. INT. NIGHT. THE BOOT ROOM. 1968.

COX, *bare-arsed and whimpering, his shaven crotch smeared black with boot polish, is being bustled and hauled up the stairs by* MOUNT, HARROP, JOYCE *and the others.*

67. INT. NIGHT. CORRIDOR. 1968.

COX, *stumbling, harassed by the others, is hustled and pushed through the darkened house.*

68. INT. NIGHT. TOWEL ROOM AND SHOWER ROOM. 1968.

In the towel room JOYCE *hauls out a laundry basket and empties it of its soiled contents.*

COX: Oh please, Mount. No. Please don't, Mount. I swear I—

(MOUNT *cracks* COX *savagely on the top of his head with his knuckles.* COX *staggers under the blow, covers his aching skull with his hands.*)

MOUNT: Shut up, creep!

(COX *is flung into the empty laundry basket and the straps are buckled down. The basket is then dragged into the shower room and set beneath a shower which is then turned on.*

The others stand and watch the basket being drenched with the cold water, highly pleased with themselves.)

HARROP: That fixed him.

MOUNT: Little bastard, smoking like that.

COLENSO: Little spastic.

MOUNT: Fixed his bloody smoking, that's what.

(*Laughter.*)

JOYCE: God, I hate that guy.

MOUNT: Hate his sodding guts.

(*They slowly leave the shower room, with a few backward glances and muttered insults.*)

69. INT. NIGHT. TOWEL ROOM. 1968.

CU NILES *standing in the shadows looking into the shower room.*

70. INT. NIGHT. SHOWER ROOM. 1968.

NILES*'s POV: The laundry basket beneath the shower. The battering sound of the water on the wicker basket.*

NILES *steps forward and pulls the basket out from beneath the shower. He unbuckles the straps and lifts the top up.*

Shot of COX *huddling fearfully in the basket.*

NILES: Get out, Cox. You can go.

(COX *gets out uncertainly, suspecting a trap. He is sopping wet.*)

COX: What?

NILES: You can go. Clear off. Get back to bed.

COX (*still confused*): Oh.

NILES: Well, go on then.

COX: Oh, right . . . I'm just a bit . . . Thanks, Niles. It was—

NILES (*pushes him*): Go on. Piss off.

COX: Thanks, Niles. I—

NILES (*Pushing him, almost sending him sprawling. Angrily*): Bugger off out of it, you little runt.

(COX *backs out of the shower room. CU of his face. Mix to Scene 71.*)

71. INT. NIGHT. COX'S BEDSIT. 1978.

COX *laboriously filling a sock with stones, sand and gravel. He knots it, then tests his cosh gently on the palm of his hand. Then he gets to his feet and suddenly and furiously smashes it down on the table top, once, twice, three times as hard as he can. CU of his face, intense, troubled and plainly a little mad.*

72. EXT. NIGHT. LANE NEAR MOUNT'S HOUSE. 1978.

MOUNT's *Volvo driving down lane.*

73. INT. NIGHT. MOUNT'S CAR. 1978.

MOUNT's *POV: Headlights pick out a bicycle abandoned in the middle of the road, rear wheel spinning.*

74. EXT. NIGHT. LANE. 1978.

Car stops and MOUNT *gets out. He looks around, then picks up the bicycle and pushes it to the verge at the side of the road.*

COX *bursts suddenly from the bushes, wielding his cosh, and
knocks* MOUNT *to the ground.*
MOUNT *is badly stunned and fails to get to his feet.*
COX *kicks him viciously. Then* COX *goes through* MOUNT's
pockets and removes his wallet. Then he walks back to the car.

75. INT. NIGHT. MOUNT'S CAR. 1978.

COX *searching the car. He goes through the glove compartment
and finds the gun.*
He smiles.
Suddenly he's jerked backward out of the car.

76. EXT. NIGHT. LANE. 1978.

COX *and* MOUNT *(woozy, blood on face) fight scrappily.*
MOUNT *is still too stunned to be effective.* COX *hits* MOUNT
another glancing blow on the head with his sap.
MOUNT *slumps to his knees, tries to grab hold of* COX.
COX *kicks himself clear and runs away into the woods.*
MOUNT, *groaning, groggily gets to his feet.*

77. INT. DAY. NILES'S FLAT. 1978.

NILES *sitting alone in his flat. For once there is no reggae. On
the floor by his feet is a bag containing cricket gear.*
NILES *seems lost in aimless thought. Then he looks up suddenly.*
He goes to the window and looks out.

78. EXT. DAY. THE STREET. 1978.

NILES's *POV: A brief flash of an indistinct figure in a white
coat walking out of sight.*

79. INT. DAY. NILES'S FLAT. 1978.

CU NILES *frowning slightly. He walks slowly back to his seat and picks up his cricket gear.*

80. INT. DAY. CRICKET PAVILION. 1978.

FRANCES, *smoking worriedly.*
NILES *comes in.*
NILES: Sorry I'm late. (*Sees* FRANCES) Oh, hello. I didn't—
FRANCES: Alisdair's been mugged.
NILES: *What!*
FRANCES: Last night. About half-ten.
NILES: Good God! Is he . . . ? Jesus. Where?
FRANCES: In the lane near our house.
NILES: Jesus. (*Pause.*) Listen, Frances, I've got to see you.
FRANCES (*a little hysterically*): For God's sake, don't bother
    me with that now.
NILES: I'm sorry, I've got to . . . Frances, I want—
MOUNT: Not interrupting anything, am I?
    (MOUNT'*s head is bandaged.*)
NILES (*stepping back*): No, no. Just fixing a tennis lesson.
    Jesus, Alisdair, how are you feeling?
MOUNT (*to* FRANCES): Look after these for me, will you,
    darling? (*Hands her some car keys.*)
    (NILES *looks at* FRANCES.)
MOUNT (*coolly*): Don't worry. It looks worse than it is. Just
    a couple of stitches. Bastard stole my wallet.
NILES: You're not thinking of playing, are you?
MOUNT: Course I'm bloody playing. I'm not missing my
    cricket for some bloody social deviant.
    (HARROP *looks through the pavilion door.*)
HARROP: Of course he's playing, Wog. How's tricks,
    Alisdair?
MOUNT: No problems.

HARROP: We're batting. Jesus, haven't you changed yet, Wog? Get a move on.

MOUNT: See you outside. (*To* FRANCES, *in reassuring but ironic tones*) I'm fine, darling. Absolutely fine. Don't you worry your little self. (*He leaves with* HARROP.)

NILES: Christ, are you sure? I mean is he OK enough to?

FRANCES (*bitterly*): There's absolutely nothing *I* can do about it anyway. Fat chance. No if he wants to play his cricket . . . Play up, play up—you know the routine.

NILES: I can't get over it.

FRANCES (*softly*): The gun's gone.

NILES: What?

FRANCES: They went through the car. They took the gun as well.

NILES (*passes hand across forehead*): Oh, Jesus.

FRANCES: You didn't mention . . . ?

NILES: Me? God no. Not a word. No, no.

FRANCES: Thank God for that. (*Pause.*) That's something. One of those things, then. (*She looks him in the eye.*)

NILES: Yes.

FRANCES: An unpleasant coincidence, then.

NILES: Yes. I suppose so. Yes.

(*Shouts from outside. "Come on, Wog," "Where's the opening bat?"*

NILES *and* FRANCES *look at each other.*)

81. EXT. DAY. CRICKET PITCH. 1978.

NILES *and* MOUNT *going in to open the batting.*
Great cheers for MOUNT *from the other members of the team.*
NILES *looks around at the others, then* NILES *claps too, bat on glove.*
MOUNT *goes to crease and takes guard.*
NILES *at the other end, looking around the field.*

NILES's *POV: scan ground, focus on empty bench.*

82. EXT. DAY. CRICKET PITCH. 1978.

Shot of scoreboard. MOUNT 16, NILES 3.
Cut to NILES *playing a stroke. He takes an easy single.*
At the other end NILES *removes his gloves and wipes his sweaty face. He looks around him unconcernedly. Then his face stiffens.*
NILES's *POV: a long shot of a small figure in a white mackintosh sitting on a bench.*
Cut back to NILES.
NILES (*softly*): Oh, Christ, no.
  (*Long shot of* COX *getting to his feet and advancing steadily on to the pitch. At first he's not noticed.*
  Camera moves in on COX. *He walks past a* FIELDER.)
FIELDER: Hey! Get off the bloody pitch.
  (COX *ignores him.*
  The FIELDER *advances on* COX. *Shouts from the pavilion—*
  "*Get off the bloody pitch.*"
  Cut to other players, including MOUNT *and* NILES, *looking around at the commotion.*
  The players adopt attitudes of resigned tolerance—as if interrupted by a streaker or a clown—hands on hips, heads shaking tiredly.
  Cut back to the FIELDER.)
FIELDER (*grabbing* COX): Get off the pitch, you bloody yokel.
  (COX *frenziedly shakes him off, draws the gun from his coat pocket and fires a warning shot into the air.*
  There is instant panic.
  Everyone is galvanized. Screams and shouts.
  The FIELDER *backs rapidly off.*
  COX *turns and marches on, waving the gun awkwardly, a mad possessed figure.*

Cut to CU of NILES's *horrified face.*
Cut back to COX.)

COX: MOUNT!

(*He whirls around to confront three fielders who had been creeping up on him from behind.*
He fires two wild shots.
The entire fielding team scatters and falls to the ground.
People race off to the boundary.
Only NILES *and* MOUNT *are left at the wicket.* COX *approaches.*)

COX: MOUNT!

NILES (*shouting*): Run, Alisdair! Run!

(*CU of* MOUNT's *face. A moment of panicky indecision.*
Then he turns, flings his bat at the advancing COX *and runs off as best he can in his pads.*
COX *starts immediately to run after him screaming crazily.*
He fires once, and a puff of dust leaps up in front of MOUNT. *He frantically starts weaving to and fro.*
Cut to NILES *looking at them. CU his face.*
Pause.
Then suddenly he starts to run after them.
Cut to COX *who whirls around and fires wildly at* NILES.
NILES *dives to the ground.*
Cut back to COX *who tears after the lumbering* MOUNT, *ungainly in his pads.* COX *fires again.*
Cut to MOUNT *who falls, screaming, hit in the back of his thigh.*
Cut to COX, *who gives a triumphant shout of delight. He runs up to* MOUNT *who is crawling futilely for the boundary.*
COX *drops to his knees and cruelly thrusts the snout of his gun into* MOUNT's *ear.*
CU of COX's *deranged joyous face.*)

COX (*low voice*): Got you. Got you, you bastard. It's me, Cox. Cox. Cox has got you, you bastard.

(CU MOUNT *gibbering, squirming in pain and fear.*
Cut to a CU of the hammer of the colt being drawn back.)
COX: Ready? We've got punishments for people like you.
(*Bends down to whisper in his ear*) A special category of
punishment for wankers like you, Mount. I'm going
to kill you, Mount. That's the punishment. Removal
of life. You've got ten seconds left. Ten seconds
before it's removed. Think about it, Mount. Think
about me, Cox. Me doing this to you. Ten seconds
left. Ten, nine . . . (*He slowly rises to his feet, the pistol
leveled.*)
Cut immediately to NILES *lying on the ground.*
NILES's *POV:* COX *and* MOUNT *some twenty yards away.*
COX *with his back slightly turned toward* NILES, *standing
above* MOUNT's *prostrate body, the gun pointing at his head.*
NILES *can see* COX's *lips moving but can't hear what's being
said.*
Cut back to NILES.
NILES *looks about him desperately.*
NILES's *POV: sees abandoned cricket ball.*
NILES *looks back at* COX *and* MOUNT *as if evaluating a
possible course of action. Then he scrambles over to the ball.
He picks it up and gets to his feet.*
Cut to his POV of COX *and* MOUNT. *Then draw back to
include* NILES *preparing to throw.*
Brief CU of his sweating concentrating face.
Beat.
NILES *hurls the ball full strength (perhaps a sudden silent
slow motion sequence.* NILES's *throw is all power and
elegance, he puts everything he has into it).*
Cut to COX. *The ball glances off his back. He lets out a cry
of pain and spins around.*
Cut to COX's *POV:* NILES *advancing on him, cricket bat
held like a club.*)
COX (*baffled and astonished, screaming*): What are you doing?

Are you mad? What do you think you're doing?
(*Cut to* NILES *advancing.*)

COX (*screaming*): You're with me! You're with me!
(*Cut to* NILES. *He clubs* COX *with the bat. He hits him a glancing blow on the head.*

COX *staggers wildly, his body suddenly twitching crazily out of control. The gun drops from his hand.*

COX *looks at* NILES *uncomprehendingly.*

Cut to a CU of NILES's *fixed agonized face. Then* NILES *ruthlessly clubs him again. The bat smashes into the side of* COX's *head and sends him flying.*

COX *hits the ground in a crumpled heap and stays there. Immediately there are shouts as people start to stream in from the boundary.*

Cut to NILES *standing above the slavering and petrified* MOUNT.)

NILES (*expressionlessly*): It's all right, Alisdair. It's all right. I got him. (*Slowly* MOUNT *grasps this fact. He looks up and sees* COX's *crumpled body.*

NILES *helps* MOUNT *turn over and lays him on his back.*

NILES *stands up and looks over at* COX.

Cut to COX.

Cut to NILES.

Cut to MOUNT)

MOUNT (*sobbing with gratitude and relief*): Oh God. Oh God, thank you, Woggy. Thank you, Wog. Thank you so much.

CU NILES's *face. He looks from* MOUNT *to* COX.

The other members of the team arrive. Ad-lib congratulation to NILES, *concern and worry to* MOUNT.

NILES *has his back pounded.*

We hear: "Amazing, Woggy," "Unbelievable," "Do you think it's the IRA?", "Get a doctor."

Cut to COX's *unconscious face. Blood trickles from his ear.*

Cut back to NILES's *frozen expression. He looks about him for* FRANCES.

Cut to FRANCES *as she runs up. She pauses, then crouches by* MOUNT, *takes his head in her lap.*

Cut to NILES *looking at her.*

Cut to FRANCES. *Imperceptibly she shakes her head.*

Cut to a CU of NILES*'s face.*

Slowly pull back away from the scene.

A babbling excited crowd surrounds MOUNT *and* NILES.

Some people curiously and nervously examine COX*'s body.*

NILES *walks away.*

Pull back. Fade down babble of voices to total silence.

Hold on long shot of the scene. Freeze frame.

Then, very loud, "Badge" by Cream.

Fade to black.

Credits.

THE END

Dutch Girls

A London Weekend Television production. Executive producer: Nick Elliott. Produced by Sue Birtwistle. Directed by Giles Foster.

MOLE	Bill Paterson
TRUELOVE	Colin Firth
LYNDON	Timothy Spall
DUNDINE	James Wilby
FFORDE	Daniel Chatto
CONE	Robert Addie
ROOTE	Michael Parkhouse
MURRAY	Adrian Lukis
SIMON	Christopher Beaumont
THORNTON	Guy Manning
LAMB	Hywel Williams Ellis
MKWELA	Colin McFarlane
MacGREGOR	Ian Michie
HEADMASTER	John Wells
ROMELIA	Gusta Gerritsen
GREETJE	Silvia Millecam
MRS. VAN DER MERWE	Anne Wil Blankers
MR. VAN DER MERWE	Erik Plooyer
KEES VAN DER MERWE	Richard Torn
ANNA VAN DER MERWE	Stephanie Verwijmeren
MR. ASHBEE	David Neville
BOY WITH BELL	Alex Lowe
FRENCH GIRLS	Catherine Chevalier
	Octavia Taten
DISC JOCKEY	Jeffrey Vanderbyl
GUITARIST	Andrew Dickson
FIRST PROSTITUTE	Anna Bergman
SECOND PROSTITUTE	Mitzi Mueller

1. EXT. NIGHT. SCHOOL HOUSE.

Strathdonald School, in a remote part of Scotland, at night.
Windows glow. The sky is lowering, dark.

2. INT. NIGHT. SCHOOL WORKSHOP.

Large empty dark workshop. Moonlight through windows. Pan
around the benches, lathes, tools, etc. The door opens slowly.
TRUELOVE *enters cautiously. Something bulks beneath his coat.*
He looks around, listens and switches on a lamp over a bench.

3. INT. NIGHT. SCHOOL HALLWAY.

Small hallway at the foot of some stairs. A ripped green baize
noticeboard on a wall, scratched paint, worn lino. A cold mean-
looking place. On the floor is a large handbell, brass with a
wooden handle. A BOY *approaches, picks it up and gives it a*
vigorous ring. The BOY *bellows at the top of his voice.*
BOY: Ten minutes to first lights out!

4. INT. NIGHT. SCHOOL WORKSHOP.

Very distant sound of the bell.
TRUELOVE'S *intent face: he looks up momentarily. Then he*

III

*resumes his task, grunting slightly from the effort as he tightens
something.*
*Extreme CU of a vice with an indeterminate curved piece of
wood clamped in it.*

5. INT. NIGHT. SCHOOL DORMITORY.

FFORDE, *head boy, patrols a dormitory.*
FFORDE: So where's Truelove?
MACGREGOR: Under the bed.
FFORDE: Jellicoe—where's Truelove?
LYNDON: In t' bog.

6. INT. NIGHT. SCHOOL SHOWER ROOM.

*Empty shower room—gray wet concrete, stark tiled walls. A
single cold shower is running. A small* BOY *in full running gear
jogs miserably on the spot beneath it, his teeth chattering.*
DUNDINE *(in blazer and flannels) watches him from a safe
distance; he checks his watch.*
DUNDINE *(all languid irony)*: Only three more minutes,
      Dawes. Cheer up.

7. INT. NIGHT. SCHOOL WORKSHOP.

CU TRUELOVE's *face, tongue between teeth. The shrill buzzing
sound of an electric saw.*
*CU piece of wood. The saw's blade cutting away a section of it.
Sawdust flies.*

8. INT. NIGHT. MOLE's ROOM.

A small neat bedsit. The distant sound of a bell.
BOY *(VO)*: First lights out!
      (MOLE, *the games master, humming to himself, polishes his*

shoes *vigorously. On the walls of the room are many
reproductions of famous Van Goghs.* MOLE *pauses, looks up
at them. His face goes wistful, dreamy.*)

9. INT. NIGHT. SCHOOL WORKSHOP.

*CU of a small metal pan bubbling thickly over a Bunsen burner.
It is filled with molten lead.*
TRUELOVE *adds some more lead nuggets. Then he returns to the
vice.*
*CU his hands gouging out a hole in the block of wood with a
chisel.*
*He carefully pours the molten lead into the hollow he has made
in the piece of wood. Hiss and smoke as the lead hits the wood.*
TRUELOVE *flinches.*

10. INT. NIGHT. DORMITORY.

FFORDE: Night, girls.
BOYS: Night.

11. INT. NIGHT. SCHOOL WORKSHOP.

TRUELOVE *binding the piece of wood with wire. He does this
neatly and professionally with pliers. Then he binds rubber
insulating tape over the wire. He pauses, finished.*
CU his face, flushed, sweaty.
*Pull back to discover that the piece of wood is the head of a
hockey stick.*
TRUELOVE *stands up and weighs the stick in his hands. It is
manifestly heavier. A slow smile of satisfaction spreads across his
face.*
*Pull back as he takes a few practice swings. Then, explosively he
lashes out at mid-air as if the stick is a club and he is being*

attacked by invisible assailants. He pauses, panting, then switches out lamp and leaves.

12. EXT. DAY. SCHOOL.

Exterior shot of the school. We see four boys in running gear run into school building.

13. INT. DAY. WASHROOM.

The washroom is empty. Rows of basins, duckboards on the floor. Urinal trough in the background. TRUELOVE *stands at a basin with his shirt off, about to shave. There is a clamor of background noise: shouts, footsteps, pop music.* TRUELOVE *uncertainly sprays shaving cream on to his hand, as if he's not really sure what he's doing. He starts spreading it on his face. He holds up the razor.* CONE *and* ROOTE *come in at this juncture.* CONE *wears a Walkman. Does a histrionic double-take. Points incredulously at* TRUELOVE.

CONE (*removing headphones*): Good God. (*Shouts*) Truelove's shaving, everyone! Jesus. Didn't you have a shave last week?

(TRUELOVE *ignores him.*)

ROOTE (*basso profundo*): *Wow.* Virile, Shave-a-day Truelove.

(TRUELOVE *turns, foam all over his face, and waggles two fingers at them both. He returns to his shaving. He moves the razor very gingerly.*)

CONE: Rasp, rasp.

ROOTE (*mock-Shakespearian*): The steely bristles yielded reluctantly to the advancing blade.

(TRUELOVE *ignores them, continues with his laborious shave.*)

ROOTE: Come on. Let's leave the *man* to his task.

CONE: Oh, by the way, Dundine told us to tell you that the team was up.

TRUELOVE (*jerks at this news*): Ow! (*Cuts himself.*) Bloody sods! (*He grabs a towel and races out of the washroom.* CONE *and* ROOTE *laugh delightedly.*)

14. INT. DAY. CORRIDOR.

TRUELOVE, *running wildly down the corridor, pulling on a blazer over hastily donned shirt and tie. Shaving foam still on his face. He swerves and dodges boys in the corridor.*
MURRAY *flattens himself against the wall to let him by, then, smiling, shouts.*
MURRAY: No running in corridors!
    (TRUELOVE *ignores him.*)

15. INT. DAY. CLOISTERS.

A small group of boys, seniors and juniors, gathered around a noticeboard. TRUELOVE *barges through them.*
Cut to the notice on the noticeboard.
CU heading: "First XI Hockey Tour to Amsterdam."
Cut to TRUELOVE. *Desperately worried look, blood trickling from his shaving cut.*
CU his finger running down list.
CU the name "TRUELOVE N. P."
Cut to TRUELOVE, *his face transformed with relief and joy. He backs off. He collapses slowly, as if he's fainted. Raises hands in attitude of prayer.*
TRUELOVE: Thank you, God. Thank you, thank you, thank you.
DUNDINE: Told you you'd make it, didn't I? No sweat.
TRUELOVE: Christ I was worried, Phil. I thought Bucknell would get picked for sure.
DUNDINE: Yeah, but he didn't have the magic stick, did he?
TRUELOVE: No.

DUNDINE: And now Amsterdam. Venice of the North.
  Away from this Godforsaken spot.
TRUELOVE: My God, Amsterdam.
DUNDINE: Amsterbloodydam. Think of them—waiting for
  us. All those Dutch girls . . . eh?

16. INT. DAY. HEADMASTER'S STUDY.

The study is large, comfortably appointed, soft armchairs and
settee, team photos, an oar above the mantelpiece. The
HEADMASTER, *in dark green tweeds, stands in front of his desk, a*
pipe in his mouth. He is very confident, sure in his role, and
exudes a certain smug authority. At his side, unbelievably spruce,
ramrod stiff, is MOLE.
HEADMASTER: Right, gentlemen. I've called you here today
  primarily to wish you all luck in this very exciting
  tour on which you are about to embark.
  (*He is interrupted by* LYNDON *entering, with a crash, in full*
  goal-keeping gear.)
HEADMASTER: Why are you dressed like that, Jellicoe?
LYNDON: Sorry, Sir. Thought—thought we had a practice,
  Sir. You know, last minute sort of thing . . . Sir,
  sorry.
MOLE: I'll see you after. Very ignorant boy, Headmaster.
  Very, very stupid.
MURRAY: Sir.
HEADMASTER: Yes.
MURRAY: Excuse me, Sir, but where will we be staying?
HEADMASTER (*suddenly very angry*): I am coming to that.
  Will you kindly not interrupt!
MURRAY: Sir.
HEADMASTER: If all goes well there may be more ventures
  of this kind. Tennis teams perhaps. Athletics in the
  summer—will you stop doing that, Thornton! . . .
  The upshot of this is that you all carry a heavy

responsibility. I want you to look on yourselves as ambassadors. You will be representing your country—Strathdonald School—if you succeed, an embassy will be built in the hearts of the good people of Heemdaam Gymnasium.

Now, I want to make one thing absolutely clear, fully understood, Mr. Mole's word is law. He will be assisted in his endeavors by your Captain, Giles, who will be Mr. Mole's right hand. (FFORDE *reluctantly steps forward.*)

Now it only remains for me to emphasize that you are not, repeat not, about to embark on your holidays. I don't care whether you're in London, or Amsterdam, or Rotterdam or Timbuktu, as far as I am concerned you are still at school.

17. EXT. DAY. SCHOOL HOUSE.

A bus is parked on the edge of a graveled forecourt, some distance away from the main door. The boys stand sullenly around piles of kit and hockey sticks and cases. Some listlessly hit hockey balls to each other.

BOY (*VO*): Mkwela! Stop fooling around, you two. Come on, get this lot loaded up.

DUNDINE: Total disaster.

TRUELOVE: I don't see.

MURRAY: What girl is going to look at us in this get-up, you daft prat.

DUNDINE: Can you see yourself going into a bar in this gear? "Pint of milk please, mister, oh and a ribena chaser." Makes you want to puke. I've got a bagful of clothes too . . . Oh my God, look at Lyndon. It's a hard life being a millionaire's son.

MURRAY: Great Yorkshire git.

(LYNDON *has changed back into his uniform, but is wearing a lurid yellow and brown shirt.*)

18. INT. DAY. STAFF ROOM.

Large, well-used room. Assorted second-hand sofas and armchairs. Large noticeboard covered in notices, lists, timetables, etc. Table with tea and coffee equipment. On one wall a set of pigeonholes stuffed with magazines, exam papers, exercise books, etc. A few masters lounge in chairs. A couple read papers.
MOLE *enters carrying suitcase, spruce in a tightly belted raincoat. Pauses as if for a reaction. None is forthcoming. He changes course and makes for the pigeonholes, reaches up.*
CU his pigeonhole ("A. McL. MOLE") quite empty.
CU MOLE's *face: wry smile.*
His fingers briefly drumming in the empty pigeonhole.
He turns and makes for the door.
The other masters chat and read as if he isn't there.
MOLE: Well . . . Cheerio . . . (*clears throat*) ah cheerio . . .
    I'll be off . . . (*gestures*) Amsterdam . . . yes (*nods*)
    well . . .
    (*He backs to the door as he speaks, gives a swift half-wave and lets himself out.*
    A master looks around in mildest curiosity.
    The door, closing.)

19. EXT. DAY. SCHOOL HOUSE.

The boys board the bus.
BOY (*VO*): Hurry up, you horrible little animal.
BOY (*VO*): Out of my way, smell.
LAMB: Take your stick, Truelove?
TRUELOVE: What? Oh, um, no. I'll hang on to it, thanks.
    (*He shoots a glance at* DUNDINE. *Throughout the film*

TRUELOVE *is rarely parted from his stick.*
MOLE *and* FFORDE *emerge from school house.*)
MOLE: Right, everyone on the coach, sharpish. Milk it,
   milk it. (*He sees* LYNDON'*s shirt.*) Good God. Jellicoe.
   Come here, laddie. Come here at once. Like, what has
   got into you, Jellicoe. What's going on here? Is it solid
   bone? Just rock solid up here?
LYNDON: Sorry, Sir. I'll just get on the bus, Sir.
MOLE: Didn't you hear what the Headmaster said?
LYNDON: Yeah. We're ambassadors like, and we'll build an
   embassy in a gymnasium, Sir.
MOLE: School uniform, you dooley. Regulation school
   uniform. This is not Hawaiian Five-Oh! Fforde, get
   him another shirt. (*To* LYNDON) Off!
   (FFORDE *gets into bus.*)

20. INT. DAY. BUS.

LYNDON (*VO*): *Sir.*
FFORDE: OK, who's got a spare shirt for Lyndon?
CONE: Angelface has got one.
LAMB: I bloody haven't.
CONE: You bloody have.
   (CONE *and* ROOTE *tear open* LAMB'*s bag, find a shirt and
   throw it to* FFORDE.)
LAMB: Bastards!
CONE *and* ROOTE (*falsetto*): Bastards!

21. EXT. BUS. DAY.

LYNDON, *fingers on nipples, acting coquettishly. Loud laughter
from the others.*
MOLE (*VO*): You're as thick as . . . Cut that out, Jellicoe!
BOY (*VO*): Wor, look at those tits.
   (FFORDE *hands the shirt to* LYNDON.)

FFORDE (*over* MOLE*'s shoulder sees* HEADMASTER *emerge from front door*): I think the Headmaster's coming, Sir.
(*Cut to smiling* HEADMASTER *emerging from front door.*)
MOLE (*looking around*): Hell's teeth! Come on, Jellicoe. Get on the bus. Come on. Milk it, man. (*To driver*) Adiamo, adiamo . . . Hector, schnell, schnell! To the station, man, quickly! Milk it!
(*Cut to* HEADMASTER*'s POV as* LYNDON, *carrying shirt and blazer, and* FFORDE *are bustled on to the bus.*
MOLE *jumps in after them.*
There's a crunch of gears and, spitting gravel from under its rear wheels, the bus roars off.)
HEADMASTER (*bellowing at bus*): Come back. There is a naked boy on that bus. Mr. Mole! Mr. *Mole!*

22. EXT. NIGHT. EDINBURGH STATION.

We hear Edinburgh station announcements. The team strides strongly up the platform, line abreast. MOLE *is in the middle. The boys are excited, full of anticipation. Other passengers dodge and scurry out of their way.* LYNDON *wears* LAMB*'s shirt—skintight, the buttons straining across his chest.*

23. INT. NIGHT. MOLE AND FFORDE'S COMPARTMENT.

MOLE *and* FFORDE *entering their compartment.*
MOLE: Right, Fforde. Top bunk for you. (*Slings his grip on to bottom bunk.*)
FFORDE: Sorry, Sir. I can't sleep in the top bunk.
MOLE: Well that's too bad, Fforde. "Tough luck." "Hard cheddar."
FFORDE: No, Sir. It makes me sick. (*He gestures at the bunks*) Wouldn't be very nice for you down below, Sir.
(*Grudgingly, and with heavy suspicion,* MOLE *clambers up to the top bunk, tests it out. He looks very uncomfortable.*

There's a lurch as the train moves off and he cracks his head on a protruding shelf.)
MOLE: Ow! God! (*Hits shelf*) Bastard!
FFORDE (*innocently*): Everything OK, Sir?

24. EXT. NIGHT. EDINBURGH STATION.

The train pulling out of the station. The boys hang out of the windows. MURRAY *unfurls a toilet roll.* CONE *and* DUNDINE *flash V-signs at train spotters.* LAMB *gives a "Sieg Heil." The others shout ribald comments to each other.* LYNDON *lets off a fire extinguisher.*

25. INT. NIGHT. SLEEPING COMPARTMENT.

DUNDINE *and* TRUELOVE's *compartment.* TRUELOVE *sitting on bottom bunk.* DUNDINE *standing in front of the mirror elaborately combing hair.*
TRUELOVE: Do you really think there's some chance with these Dutch girls?
DUNDINE: You've got to make your own chances, Neil.
TRUELOVE: Yeah . . .
DUNDINE: You can't just sit back and wait. Think someone will come along and say, "Hey, I like you. Let's make the earth move, baby."
TRUELOVE: Right.
DUNDINE: Don't worry, Neil. Leave it to me. I'll get you a girl.
TRUELOVE: Jesus.

26. INT. NIGHT. MOLE AND FFORDE's COMPARTMENT.

FFORDE *in bed pretending to read.* MOLE *finishes brushing his teeth in the small basin (much hawking and spitting, rinsing and gargling).*

FFORDE *looks pained.*

MOLE *is wearing very old-fashioned striped pajamas.*

MOLE (*spitting*): Ever seen that film, Fforde? (*Gargles*) Lust for Life? (*Final spit*) Starring Kirk Davis. (*As he climbs the ladder to his bunk*) Superb actor. Superb . . . (*gestures*) wonderful film . . . One of the greats. (*Pained, suffering expression. Settling down with Van Gogh book.*) Remember that bit, Fforde? That very nasty business with the ear . . . when he . . . (*goes through the motions*) slices it off and gives it to the . . . to the . . . the prostitute.

FFORDE: What, Sir?

MOLE (*incredulous at* FFORDE'*s ignorance*): What, Sir? Vincent Van Gogh and his ear.

FFORDE (*deeply bored*): Sorry, Sir, Van who?

> (MOLE *leans over bunk.*
> FFORDE'*s POV as* MOLE'*s upside-down head appears.* FFORDE *gives a little yelp of shock.*)

MOLE (*upside down*): Vincent Van Gogh, that's who, Fforde.

FFORDE: Oh. Van *Goh*. Vincent Van Goh.

MOLE (*disgusted*): Van *Goh*. Van Goghchchch. Van Goghchchch, Fforde. (FFORDE *flinching from the shower of spittle, looking pained.*)

FFORDE: Sorry, Sir.

27. INT. NIGHT. DUNDINE AND TRUELOVE'S COMPARTMENT.

MURRAY *comes in.*

DUNDINE: Hi, Jub-Jub.

MURRAY: Have you got your stuff? Ace. Well, let's go.

DUNDINE: OK, Neil, the tour starts here.

MURRAY: Whahey! Let's party!

28. INT. NIGHT. NIGHT CORRIDOR.

MURRAY, TRUELOVE, DUNDINE *walking down corridor. They go past* MOLE'*s compartment on tiptoe.*
They pause at a door. MURRAY *gives a special knock. The door opens. A great cloud of smoke billows out as if something is burning inside. The boys go in.*

29. INT. NIGHT. ROOTE'S COMPARTMENT.

Inside, crammed into every inch of available space are CONE, ROOTE, LAMB, SIMON, MKWELA, THORNTON, MacGREGOR *and* LYNDON.
Everyone is smoking and the compartment is dim and choking in the fug. Bottles of booze and cans of beer are scattered around and various sex magazines are being circulated, their centerfolds inspected. It looks like a very crowded, very low-budget orgy. Cheers as DUNDINE, TRUELOVE *and* MURRAY *enter. They settle down.*

DUNDINE: Goodbye Scotland, hello life.
  (*More cheers.*)
  Let's see a bloody nude book then. Christ, you're not allowed to look at these white girls, Benny. (*He snatches a magazine from* MKWELA.)
MKWELA: Sorry, baas. (*He snatches a magazine from* LYNDON.)
ROOTE: (*looking at magazine*) God, she's nice. (*Groans as if in intense pain.*) "Andrea, aged seventeen from Birmingham." Christ, seventeen! I don't know *any* girl who looks like that.
THORNTON: If she's seventeen, I'll eat my hat. Whompers that size? Never.
SIMON: Ah, the expert speaks.
MKWELA: But what about me though? I mean, I bet your Dutch girls don't like darkies.
MURRAY: No, you'll be all right, Benny. They're quite—"tolerant" in Holland.

ROOTE: All I pray is that just this once my opposite number has a beautiful sister. A beautiful sixteen-year-old . . .
MURRAY: Or a beautiful mother, dissatisfied with her overweight husband . . .
(*There's a knock on the door. Immediate silence.*)
ROOTE: Jesus! Lights Out!
(*The lights are switched out. Another knock.*)
ROOTE (*faking drowsiness*): Wha . . . Who'sat? What is it?
(*Stifled giggles from the others. Cigarettes glow in the dark.*)

30. INT. NIGHT. TRAIN CORRIDOR.

FFORDE *outside in the passage. He looks very worried.*
FFORDE (*with relief*): Thank God . . . it's me, Giles.

31. INT. NIGHT. ROOTE'S COMPARTMENT.

Cut back to compartment. Cigarette ends glow in the darkness. Cut to ROOTE. *Everyone tries not to laugh.*
ROOTE: Um, look, Giles, ah, I'm afraid it's a tiny bit awkward at the moment.

32. INT. NIGHT. TRAIN CORRIDOR.

Cut to FFORDE.
FFORDE: Come on, James, open up.

33. INT. NIGHT. ROOTE'S COMPARTMENT.

Cut to ROOTE.
ROOTE (*whispering*): Hell's bloody bells. What do we do?
DUNDINE: Don't worry, I'll handle Giles.
(ROOTE *opens the door.* FFORDE *comes uneasily in. The*

124

lights go on. FFORDE, *coughing furiously at the smoke, looks around him in astonishment.*)

DUNDINE: Hi, Giles.

FFORDE: Christ on a bike! Jesus, Philip . . .

DUNDINE: Just a little pretour celebration, Giles. (*Producing cigarettes*) Have a fag.

MKWELA (*offering bottle*): Scotch?

ROOTE (*offering magazine*): Nude book?

FFORDE: Jesus, you guys, this is *terrible*. (*Unthinkingly, he takes a cigarette from* DUNDINE's *proffered pack.* LYNDON *leans forward with a lighter.*) This is bloody disaster, you realize. Total hell. (*He leans forward.* LYNDON *lights his cigarette.* FFORDE *inhales deeply; he's clearly a practiced smoker. He runs his hand through his hair distractedly.*) Utter nightmare. (*He suddenly realizes what he's got in his hand. Looks at his cigarette in horror.*) Jesus, you guys, this is terrible. I'll have to turn you lot in.

MACGREGOR: Fancy a wee drop of this cream de menth?

FFORDE: Christ I don't want to do it, but . . . we've not even reached London yet . . . God Almighty. What's it going to be like on the boat?

34. EXT. DAY. STERN OF SHIP.

Come in on the wake.

DUNDINE (*VO*): God I was smashed.

TRUELOVE (*VO*): Christ, me too.

(*Pan around to* DUNDINE *and* TRUELOVE *leaning over rail.*)

DUNDINE: Still, good start to the tour. Now, bring on the girls.

TRUELOVE: Damn right.

(FFORDE *approaches, pale-faced, twitchy, distracted.*)

DUNDINE: Giles, hi. You don't look so hot. Death warmed up.

FFORDE: To tell you the truth, I feel bloody awful. (*Rubs his*

eyes.) Look, um, about what went on last night . . . I
mean, what I should have . . . or rather I *shouldn't*
have done any of, as you know. (*Twiddles hands,
shudders at the memory. Pause.*) I'm sort of going
around, you know, seeing the other guys . . . clear up
any, sort of, misunderstandings. (*His expression
changes.*) The Head . . . you see . . . (*goes into mild
shock.*) He practically swore me to celibacy for life . . .

DUNDINE (*soothingly*): Don't worry, Giles. We understand.
Absolutely no prob, Giles.
(FFORDE *nods his thanks wordlessly and stumbles off.*)
Cracking up, poor sod.
TRUELOVE: Wow.
DUNDINE: Day one.

35. INT. DAY. FERRY CORRIDOR.

A long corridor. A young GIRL—*a cleaner—pushing a trolley.
She stops at a cabin door, glances up.
Cut to* THORNTON, *case in hand, acting innocently down the
other end of the corridor.
The* GIRL *goes into the cabin.
Cut to* THORNTON, *his face transfigured with lust, as he scurries
up to the door. He looks around, then steps inside.
Pause. Hold on the door for a beat.
The sound of a ringing slap.* THORNTON's *"Ow!" He is flung
out of the cabin, crashes into the trolley. His case is flung out
after him. He picks himself up.*
THORNTON: Sorry, sorry. I thought you were someone else.

36. INT. DAY. FERRY.

LYNDON *is sitting opposite two very bored French girls, staring
intently at them. They make the odd remark to each other and
totally ignore him.*

LYNDON: You French? Parlez-vous?

FIRST FRENCH GIRL: *Fiche le con.*

LYNDON: Je suis rock singère. Je live in London.

FIRST FRENCH GIRL: *Salaud.*

LYNDON: No. London. Londres. Yeah . . . Touring . . .
  Got a gig in Amsterdam.

FFORDE (*approaching*): Um, hi there, Lyndon.

LYNDON: Hi, Giles. I'm chatting up these two birds. I think
  they're French.

FFORDE: It's about last night, Lyndon. Um, the situation
  has sort of revised itself to the, um, initial state of
  affairs. I mean . . . I'm not exonerating anyone . . .
  oh no . . . you know. But as for the future—in terms
  of future exoneration—well, that's a different matter
  altogether.

LYNDON: Er, sorry?

FFORDE: Great. Knew I could count on you.
  (*A baffled* LYNDON *watches him go. Then he turns around.
  The French girls have gone.*)

37. INT. DAY. SHIP'S LAVATORY.

CONE *and* ROOTE *smoking by open porthole.*

CONE: How much cash have you got?

ROOTE: Oh, about forty quid. Why?

CONE: I've got an idea.

ROOTE: What?

CONE: Well, the way I look at it is like this: if we don't get
  off with a Dutch girl—I mean "if," I bloody hope we
  do—but if we don't, then I reckon we should nick off
  into Amsterdam one night and get ourselves a tart.

ROOTE: Christ. What, you mean a prossie?

CONE: Of course I mean a bloody prossie. Find one, hand
  over the cash and how's your father. No hassles.

ROOTE: Jesus. Good idea. *Brilliant* idea. But how much are they, though?

CONE: Twenty quid should do it. I should think. Or thirty.

ROOTE (*thoughtfully*): Twenty quid—amazing idea.

CONE: But only if we don't get a Dutch girl . . . which we probably will.

38. EXT. DAY. HOLLAND, MAIN ROAD.

Come in on a sign saying "Amsterdam 45 km." The team bus thunders by.

39. INT. DAY. BUS

View of the passing countryside from the bus. Pan around to:
MOLE *at the front of the bus testing the microphone.*
He taps it, blows loudly into it.
Cut to the boys' faces, very bored.
Cut to MOLE.

MOLE: Testing, testing. Is this working? Testing, one, two, three. Do you hear me at the back? All right now. Right, settle down. Now pay attention. Right. Cone, Macgregor. Right. Now, we should arrive at Heemdaam Hockey Club early this evening. You will be staying at the homes of your opposite numbers. There will be a team practice at nine o'clock tomorrow, sharp. I mean sharp—Jellicoe. Now, there's only three matches, lads. The first is against our hosts, Heemdaam. Easy—a walkover. And at Heemdaam we will be liaising with Mr. Ashbee, who, some of you may remember, used to teach at Strathdonald. The second match is against some Amsterdam grammar school. And your third and your final match is against the Laren Hockey Club. Good, very, very, very good—but beatable. So, only

three matches, lads, so let's go for a hundred percent
record. Any questions, lads?
(*Cut to the boys, sullen and bored.*)
What, no questions? . . . What's up with you lot?
(*Trying to gee them up*)
What's got into you? (*Gestures outside*) That's Holland
out there . . . Les Pays Bas, Die Nederland . . .
Windmills, tulips, dykes . . .
(*Cut to boys' faces. A few glances at the countryside.*)
The birthplace of Vincent Van Gogh. (*Settles down.*)
Now, not far from here, in a small town called
Dordrecht, Van Gogh—Vincent—Vincent was a clerk
in a bookshop.
(*Cut to the boys' horror-struck faces.*)

40. EXT. DAY. BUS, HOLLAND.

The bus, traveling through the countryside. Slowly fade down
MOLE's *words.*
MOLE (*VO*): Yes. In fact Vincent worked there from
    January to April 1877 before going back to
    Amsterdam to prepare for theological college. After
    fourteen months' desperately hard study . . .

41. INT. NIGHT. BUS.

Come in on the boys, exhausted, shattered, victims of terminal
boredom. FFORDE *is just finishing handing out name badges.*
MOLE *is standing at the front of the bus, still on the mike.*
MOLE (*VO*): . . . Vincent's father very sadly died in
    Nuewnen, and it was later in that year that he painted
    his very, very famous painting *The Potato Eaters*,
    which we all know. Later that year toward the end of
    the year, he went to live in Antwerp. And I think that
    we've arrived now at the Heemdaam Hockey Club.

42. EXT. NIGHT. FLOODLIT CAR PARK.

MOLE: Now, name badges on. Try and smarten yourselves up. And try, please, to look happy to be here. All right—let's have you. Milk it, milk it.
Mr. Ashbee? Alexander . . . Sandy Mole.

ASHBEE: Welcome to Holland.
(*Behind him the boys file off the bus, collect their gear and greet their Dutch opposite numbers.*
Come in on TRUELOVE.
KEES *approaches with a slip of paper in his hand.*)

KEES: Neil Truelove?

TRUELOVE: Yes.

KEES: Kees van der Merwe.

TRUELOVE: Hello.

KEES: I have got one other. Lyndon Baines Jellicoe.

TRUELOVE: Oh no.

KEES: There are problems?

TRUELOVE: No, no. There he is. Over here.

KEES: Hello, Lyndon Baines Jellicoe.

LYNDON: It's just Lyndon. Baines is my middle name.

KEES: I am Kees van der Merwe.

LYNDON: Case? What, like, like suitcase?

KEES: Sorry? Yes, yes, take your bag to my car. Over there.

LYNDON: Jesus. You got a car?
(*They move off.*)

TRUELOVE: See you tomorrow, Phil.

MOLE (*to* ASHBEE): And this is our team captain, Giles Fforde.

ASHBEE: Hello, Giles.

FFORDE: How do you do.

ASHBEE: I was a little before your time, I think, but I knew your brother Mungo very well. How's old Mungo these days?

Dutch Girls

FFORDE: I'm afraid, he's in a sort of clinic . . .
  (KEES's *car—a jeep—passes them.* LYNDON *is standing in
  the back.*)
MOLE: Good night, Truelove, Jellicoe. Nine A.M.
  tomorrow, remember. Sharp. And, Jellicoe, no fancy
  dress . . .
  (*The jeep roars off.*)
LYNDON: Yeehah!

43. EXT. NIGHT. VAN DER MERWE HOUSE.

KEES's *car pulls up at the front door.*
LYNDON *looks at the house. It is very grand, impressive.*
LYNDON: Not too bad, Kees. Not too bad at all.

44. INT. NIGHT. VAN DER MERWE HOUSE.

TRUELOVE *and* LYNDON *led through sumptuous hallway by* KEES.
*The two English boys look around them, impressed. They go
into a drawing room, chic, elegant, tasteful. A middle-aged Dutch
couple sit on a chrome and leather sofa in front of a large color
TV. The room breathes well-heeled bourgeois comfort.*
TRUELOVE *is impressively well-mannered and charming.*
KEES: This is my mother and father. Neil Truelove.
TRUELOVE: How do you do? Very good of you to put
  us up.
  (*Cut to* LYNDON *mooching around, picking up ornaments,
  generally casing the joint.*)
MR. VAN DER MERWE: Neil, Lyndon Baines, I hope you had
  a pleasant journey.
LYNDON: It's just Lyndon. Baines is me middle name.
MR. VAN DER MERWE: I apologize.
MRS. VAN DER MERWE: Perhaps you would like to take
  your things to your room. Then we can have our
  dinner. Yes?

LYNDON: Great. I'm bloody starving.

45. INT. NIGHT. GUEST BEDROOM.

Two single beds. Another beautiful tasteful room. LYNDON *and* TRUELOVE *put their bags down.*
KEES: I will see you downstairs in five minutes. You can meet my sister then.
LYNDON: Sister?
KEES: Oh yes. In five minutes, then. (*He leaves.*)
LYNDON: Christ, not bad, eh?
(TRUELOVE *puts his bag and hockey stick down on a bed, and looks out of the window.*)
TRUELOVE: Great. My God, you should see the size of their garden.
LYNDON: This is mine.
TRUELOVE: Don't be so pathetic.
(*He removes* TRUELOVE's *bag and then picks up his stick.* TRUELOVE *darts forward too late to prevent him.* LYNDON's *eyes widen as he registers the stick's weight.*)
LYNDON: My God. You sly bastard.
(TRUELOVE, *blushing, snatches the stick from* LYNDON's *hands.*) Well, well, well, so that's how you got in the team . . . I think we've struck gold here, Neil lad. Bloody gold. And a sister. The first live Dutch girl. She's mine if she's any good, all right?
(*CU* TRUELOVE's *contemptuous face.*)

46. INT. NIGHT. DINING ROOM.

CU doorway. LYNDON *and* TRUELOVE *arrive and pause framed in it.* LYNDON *is smiling broadly. Then his face falls.*
LYNDON's *POV: the* VAN DER MERWES *at table,* MR. *and* MRS., KEES *and a little girl, about five years old.*

MRS. VAN DER MERWE: Hello. This is Anna. Say hello, Anna. To Neil and Lyndon Baines.

ANNA: Hello, English boys.

TRUELOVE (*enjoying himself*): Hello, Anna. Say hello to Anna, Lyndon Baines.

LYNDON (*sullenly*): Hello.

MRS. VAN DER MERWE: Please, sit down.

TRUELOVE: Why don't you sit beside Anna, Lyndon Baines?
(LYNDON *complies, firing* TRUELOVE *an evil look. A slice of melon is already on a plate at the places.* LYNDON *picks his up and starts eating at once.*
The VAN DER MERWES *settle down.*
Cut to LYNDON, *his mouth full of melon.*
Mix to later on in the meal. LYNDON *eating a meat dish with enormous relish and gusto, elbows out, huge mouthfuls, etc.*
Cut to TRUELOVE *trying to distract attention.*)
Um, just exactly how far are we from Amsterdam?

MRS. VAN DER MERWE: Sorry . . . Oh, let's say half an hour. (*They all look back at* LYNDON.)

TRUELOVE: Beautiful . . . lovely village. Very, ah . . .
(*Cut to* LYNDON. *His elbow is bothering* ANNA. *Impatiently she knocks it and some food jerks off* LYNDON'S *fork to splat on the table.*)

MR. VAN DER MERWE: Anna!

MRS. VAN DER MERWE: She is not accustomed to someone sitting there.

ANNA (*in Dutch*): But Mama, he eats like a pig. A big fat pig. (*She makes expressive grunting noises.*)

MRS. VAN DER MERWE (*in Dutch*): Anna, behave yourself or you'll go to your room!

ANNA (*in Dutch*): Why don't you tell him to stop eating like an animal?

LYNDON: No damage done. (*He picks the piece of meat off the table and pops it in his mouth.*) It all comes out the same

way anyway, doesn't it?
(*Cut from* LYNDON's *chomping, cheery face, to* MRS. VAN
DER MERWE's *frozen smile.*)

47. INT. NIGHT. GUEST BEDROOM.

LYNDON *in his underpants lying on his bed. The room already
looks a mess with clothes scattered here and there.* LYNDON
belches. TRUELOVE *comes in. Loud music plays on* LYNDON's
ghetto blaster.

TRUELOVE: You know that handle thing on the side of the
bog?

LYNDON: Yeah.

TRUELOVE: Well, it's got a function. You're meant to pull
it, you know. After you've crapped. It's called
"flushing."

LYNDON: Oh Christ, yeah. Sorry. I always forget to do
that for some reason. It drives my mother mad.

TRUELOVE: Well, it's bloody disgusting, I can tell you.
Bloody repellent. Christ knows what the Van Der
Merwes would think.

LYNDON: Do them good. Load of prigs.

TRUELOVE: They seem very nice to me.

LYNDON: Oh, I suppose so. *She's* a right bitch, though. I
can tell.

TRUELOVE: Mrs. Van Der Merwe?

LYNDON: No. That little sprog Anna. I just hope that all
Dutch girls won't be like her.

TRUELOVE: Well, it helps if you don't stick a sodding great
elbow in their faces.

LYNDON: That don't matter anyway. As my old man says:
"In the dark all cats are gray."
(*Pause.* TRUELOVE *looks at him.*)

TRUELOVE: Do you and your father . . . ? Talk about—you
know—that sort of thing?

LYNDON: We get on all right . . .

TRUELOVE: The only thing my father ever told me was that
"women are a lifetime's study" . . . What if he's
right? Because if he is, I've got off to a bloody slow
start.

LYNDON: Yeah—it stands to reason. When did you go to
school?

TRUELOVE: When I was seven.

LYNDON: There you are. You're like a bloody innocent
outside school. You don't know how it works.

TRUELOVE: God you can spout. I suppose you know exactly
how to handle women?

LYNDON: I just treat them like blokes. Best way.

TRUELOVE: You did really well with a five-year-old tonight.
Very impressive.

LYNDON: Well, what do you know, anyway? Have you got
any booze?

TRUELOVE: No. Dundine's got all mine.

LYNDON: Let's see what the Van Der Merwes can provide.

TRUELOVE: For God's sake, Lyndon, you can't . . .

LYNDON: They said we should make ourselves at home,
didn't they? See you later. Yeehah! (*He leaves.*
TRUELOVE's *face.*)

48. EXT. DAY. HOCKEY FIELDS.

A misty cold morning. MOLE *stands in the middle of the pitch.*

MOLE: Hit the ball, Mkwela! If you can't push it, hit it.
(MKWELA *shapes up. He attempts to hit the ball and throws
up a huge divot. The ball goes two feet.*)

MKWELA (*cheerfully*): Sorry, Sir, just can't seem to get it
right today.

MOLE: Good God. I thought your race were meant to be
naturals at this game. Born with hockey sticks in your
hands.

MKWELA: No, Sir. I think you're talking about the Indians, Sir. I'm not an Indian, Sir. I'm Nigerian, Sir, from Africa.

MOLE: Well, you may not be Indian, but you're certainly incompetent, that's for sure. Right, Truelove, you've got a good strong hit, you take the short corners.

TRUELOVE: But, Sir . . .

MOLE: Just do it, Truelove. Don't argue. Right. Ready, Roote? Dundine?

DUNDINE: Come on, Truelove.

ROOTE: Hurry up, Truelove.

MOLE: Hard, now, Truelove. Hard.

(TRUELOVE *looks at his stick.*
CU the bindings. He hits the ball. It blasts through
ROOTE'S *fingers and goes miles beyond him.*)

ROOTE: *Ow!* You bloody maniac! Practically took my fingers off.

MOLE (*furious*): You great stupid idiot! Two hours detention the first Saturday of term. (*Takes out notebook and writes punishment down.*)

TRUELOVE: Aw, Sir, come on. You said "hard."

MOLE: Not that hard, you foolish boy! Look where the bloody ball's got to. (*Gestures into the distance.*)
(*Cut to* MOLE'S *POV: we can make out small figures at the edge of the playing fields.*)

MOLE: Well, go on. Get it. Quickly! Milk it!
(TRUELOVE *jogs off through the others who sneer at him good-naturedly. The camera follows* TRUELOVE *to the ball, some thirty yards off. He picks the ball up. We hear a distant shout. He looks up.*
TRUELOVE'S *POV: six figures advancing. They are girls. There's another shout: "Hey English boys!" The girls approach. (There has to be something unreal and mystical about this shot as they advance through lingering mist drifts.)*)

Cut back to a CU of TRUELOVE's *face. He can't really believe what's happening. The ball drops from his hands. He looks back at the others, still engaged in their hockey practice, oblivious. He looks back at the girls. The shout comes again: "English boys," carrying faintly and clearly across the fields.)*

TRUELOVE: Bloody hell.

(TRUELOVE *goes hesitantly toward them. They approach. The six girls are sixteen- to eighteen-year-olds, fashionably dressed, mature-looking.* ROMELIA *and* GREETJE *among them.)*

ROMELIA: Hello, English boy.

TRUELOVE: Hello. (*Clears throat*) Hello.

(*Cut back to* MOLE *directing some exercise.)*

MOLE: Right, um, Thornton. I want you to dribble through those jerseys, then reverse pass to—
(*Cut to* CONE.)

CONE: Christ! What's Truelove doing?

(*Cut to long shot of* TRUELOVE *surrounded by girls.)*

CONE: Jesus! Bloody Truelove. That's outrageous. (*To* ROOTE) Look at that.

ROOTE: Christ Almighty! Simon, Philip, look at bloody Truelove. (CONE, ROOTE, DUNDINE *and* SIMON *slip off to join* TRUELOVE.

Cut to TRUELOVE.

ROMELIA *looks directly at* TRUELOVE.)

ROMELIA: Do you want to go to a discothèque tonight?

TRUELOVE (*sensing her interest—a little uneasy*): Who? Me?

ROMELIA: Yes, you. (*Pause.*) And your friends, of course.

TRUELOVE (*still stunned*): Oh, um, yes. I think so. Yes please.

CONE (*arriving*): Well, hello there, Neil. Aren't you going to introduce me? Morning, ladies.

ROOTE (*aside*): You shady bugger, Truelove. (*To the girls*)

Well, hello there!

(*Cut to* MOLE.)

MOLE: Okey-dokey. Now, Roote, this is where . . . Roote? Where the hell . . . ? (*Sees girls.*) Jesus H. Christ! Oh no!

(LYNDON *sees the girls.*)

LYNDON: Excuse me, Sir. I have to go to the toilet.

(*He gallops off in full goal-keeping gear to join the girls. The rest of the team follow his example.* MOLE *is left alone.*)

MOLE: Come back here! Come back here at once! (*He blows a huge blast on his whistle, sustained and shrill. His face reddens, his eyes start. When his breath gives out he reels in a swoon, staggering a bit. He pulls himself together. Choking*) You're all at school, remember . . . Not in Holland . . . at school. (*He struggles with his punishment notebook, starts writing down names. Every now and then he blows another blast on his whistle. They have no effect. He shouts threats.*

Pull back from the irate shouting figure, pan across the expanse of playing fields to the boys clustered around the girls. GREETJE *and* LYNDON *make eye contact.*)

LYNDON: Hello.

GREETJE: Hi.

LYNDON: I like your hair.

GREETJE: Oh, do you? Thank you.

MOLE (*VO*): You're all at school, remember . . . Not in Holland . . . at school. (*His subsequent threats faint in the distance.*)

49. EXT. DAY. HOCKEY PITCH.

Come in on the hands of FFORDE *and* KEES *as they exchange pennants.*

Pull back. FFORDE *and* KEES *shake hands.*

FFORDE *smiles nervously. Suddenly* KEES *punches the air and shouts "Hip!" The Dutch team respond with a "Hoi!" This is repeated twice, quickly.* FFORDE *is visibly startled. A whistle blows shrilly.*

50. EXT. DAY. HOCKEY PITCH.

The game. During snatches of hockey action . . . the Dutch team dominating . . . various conversations are interspersed. Each section ends in ball thudding into goal.

CONE: What time did they say?

ROOTE: Half-seven.

CONE: Christ, watch that bastard going through on the left!

ROOTE: Damn.

> (*Cut to* MACGREGOR *passing the ball to* MURRAY, *who's not looking.*)

MURRAY (*cheerfully*): Oh. Sorry. Sorry about that.

MACGREGOR: Fine. No problem.

> (*Cut to the ball thudding into the goal board.* LYNDON *shrugs.* MOLE's *face—incredulous.*)

MURRAY: Look, Giles, can I borrow that yellow scarf of yours?

FFORDE: For Christ's sake, Jub-Jub, we're meant to be playing a bloody match.

MURRAY: Yes or no?

FFORDE: All right, yes. God, look out, Lyndon! Shit.

> (*Cut to hockey ball striking the goal board behind* LYNDON. *He cheerfully kicks it away. Cut to* MOLE *looking heavenwards in despair. Cut back to* LYNDON.)

LYNDON: Where is this disco, anyway?

TRUELOVE: Clubhouse.

> (*A ball whistles past them and thuds into the goal board.* LYNDON's *face: as if to say, "Ah well, too bad."*
> *Cut to* MOLE—*half-time.*
> *Oranges are being passed around.*

MOLE *is outraged, he can't believe what he has witnessed.*)
MOLE: Seven-nil. Seven-nil. Come on. Where's your pride,
your spirit? I've never seen such chatter on the
field . . . Like a crowd of fishwives . . . You've got to
pull yourselves together, get those passes moving . . .
stop the bloody chit-chat. You're like a bunch of
lassies in a dress shop . . . What's all this talk about
clothes, for goodness sake? . . . Aye, *you*, Murray . . .
"Can I borrow this, can I borrow that?" Cut the
cackle, get those passes strung together, square, sharp,
crisp . . . I've never seen such a bunch of jessies . . .
yes, jessies, Cone. Look it up in the dictionary. Get
your minds on the game . . .
(*The last two-thirds of* MOLE's *half-time harangue are* VO.
*While he talks the camera moves through the boys—
completely unaffected by the pep talk—as they discuss their
plans.*)
MACGREGOR: I don't like any of them. I don't fancy any of
them.
THORNTON: Nah. Neither do I.
(Cut to MURRAY.)
MURRAY: Get a load of that one in the red.
SIMON: Mmmm. Don't go a bundle on her face . . .
MURRAY: Who's looking at faces?
(*Cut to the* GIRLS. *They smile and wave.*)
DUNDINE: Look, there she is.
TRUELOVE: Who?
DUNDINE: Romelia. (*Rolls his eyes.*
TRUELOVE's *face: troubled.*
Cut to ROMELIA: *she waves.*
Cut to DUNDINE: *he waves back. Beside him we see*
LYNDON *blow a kiss to* GREETJE.
FFORDE *edges up.*)
FFORDE: Look, Philip, about this disco thing . . .
DUNDINE: General socializing, Giles, as per the head's

instructions. Just an ordinary disco, Neil, isn't it?
(*Cut to* TRUELOVE *who is looking at* ROMELIA.)
TRUELOVE: What? Oh yes . . . just a disco. (*He smiles
reassuringly. The whistle blows for the commencement of the
second half.*)

51. INT. NIGHT. DISCO.

The clubhouse done up as a disco.
TRUELOVE *is in uniform, adapted for maximum trendiness.*
LYNDON *wears bright yellow trousers.*
Start close on ROMELIA *dancing, laughing with a group of
friends.*
At a distance TRUELOVE *and* DUNDINE *watch separately.*
ROMELIA *and* TRUELOVE *exchange looks.*
DUNDINE *puts down his drink and moves in on* ROMELIA. *They
dance. The boys dance with the girls.*
TRUELOVE *moves through the crowd to the bar where he
encounters* FFORDE *smoking and drinking.*
FFORDE: Hello, Neil. (*Waves cigarette*) I know I shouldn't,
but that game shot my nerves to hell . . . Want one?
TRUELOVE: Thanks. (*Lights cigarette.*)
FFORDE: Well, I've got my fags and my booze. Now all I
need is a girl. What about you? Weren't you going
with the blonde?
TRUELOVE: Well . . . I thought I'd . . . (*Looking around at*
DUNDINE *and* ROMELIA) . . . I haven't quite worked
things out yet.
MURRAY (*arriving*): Double bacardi and coke, please. No
luck, you two?
TRUELOVE: Give us a chance, we've only just got here.
MURRAY: Can't afford to waste time, old son. I've got one
up the back stairs there. Doesn't speak a word of
English, but she seems to like me. (*Strikes a heroic
pose.*)

ROOTE (*coming over*): I thought you said they were as passionate as the Italians, Jub-Jub.

MURRAY: I never said that. Giles did.

FFORDE: Did I? But I don't know any Italians.

LYNDON: Hello, chaps. (*He is accompanied by* GREETJE.) This is . . . ah, um, Gunge?

GREETJE: Greetje.

LYNDON (*having a stab at the pronunciation*): Sorry, Greetje. (*Looks at the others.*) Everybody having fun?
(*Mix to the dance floor later on.*
Cut to DUNDINE *and* ROMELIA *dancing.*
ROMELIA *looking around room. Waves to* TRUELOVE *and gets a listless wave in return.*
Cut to LAMB, *breakdancing and body popping energetically on his own.*
Cut to FFORDE, *drunk at the bar, smoking, talking to two Dutch girls.*)

FFORDE: See, the Headmaster said to me . . . Just before we left, took me aside. Private, friendly chat. He said to me "Giles—Giles, you're head boy, Giles, and I want you to set an example to the others." So I said to him. "Sir," I said. We have to call him Sir. "Sir," I said. "You can rely on me." (*He punches chest. Then suddenly looks appalled.*
Cut to doorway. KEES *and some of the Dutch team arrive. Friendly, happy, they greet the girls.*
Cut back to FFORDE. *He takes a huge gulp of drink and a trembling drag on his cigarette. His face twitches and his voice breaks.*)

FFORDE: But it's just not bloody fair is it? (*Sobs.*) I mean, what am I supposed to do? . . . I'm only human after all. I'm only bloody *human*. (*He starts to cry. The two girls look at him and at each other in utter astonishment.*

Cut to ROMELIA *alone at the bar. She lights a cigarette.*
TRUELOVE *approaches.)*

TRUELOVE: Hi.

ROMELIA: Hello. Are you having fun?

TRUELOVE: What? Yes, yes, I am. Great place . . . not
dancing?

ROMELIA (*looking down at herself*): No, I don't think so.

TRUELOVE: Would you, I mean—unless you . . . fancy a
dance? Only if you feel like it.

ROMELIA: Yes. (*She stubs out her cigarette.*)

TRUELOVE: Where's, um, Philip?

ROMELIA: Why? Do you need to ask his permission?
(*Cut to* TRUELOVE'*s face.*
They go onto the dance floor.)

52. INT. NIGHT. ASHBEES' DINING ROOM.

MOLE, MR. *and* MRS. ASHBEE *sitting around a dining table. The
meal is over.* MOLE *is at his most relaxed: he wears a cravat, has
combed his hair differently and puffs at a small artistic pipe (clay,
long-stemmed). He is expansive, mellow, and has clearly been
talking all evening. The* ASHBEES *are wilting.* MOLE *leans
forward, jabs pipe stem at* ASHBEE. MRS. ASHBEE *hands* MOLE *a
cup of coffee.*

MOLE: Now here's another extraordinary thing. Now I
think about it. Fascinating.

ASHBEE: Coffee, Sandy?

MOLE: Yes. Thank you. Very kind, Mrs. Ashbee. Thanks.
Now, what was I saying? Oh yes. Now, you take my
surname—Mole. You know—the wee animal, the
burrowing thing. Now, you know what the old
Scottish dialect for a mole is?

ASHBEE: I haven't the faintest notion.

MOLE: Well it's a "grockle." Now you say that quickly:

grockle. It's almost like a Dutch name. A famous Dutch name? Gogh: grockle; grockle: Gogh. See what I'm driving at? Now. What is the Dutch word for a mole?

ASHBEE: Ah, spritzmuis, I think.

MOLE: Spritzmuis? Ah well, it's just a wee theory. Vincent Van Spritzmuis. Not quite the same ring.

53. INT. NIGHT. DISCO.

CONE, ROOTE, MURRAY *and* SIMON *all looking at* LYNDON *and* GREETJE *who are kissing passionately.*

SIMON: Look at that great pill. How does he bloody do it?

MURRAY: It makes me sick.

ROOTE: Look, she's obviously nothing but a scrubber.

SIMON (*longingly*): Yeah.

(*Pause.*)

CONE: I don't call this much of a disco.

ROOTE: Dead loss.

(*Cut to* TRUELOVE *and* ROMELIA *dancing together. Music goes into a slow number.* TRUELOVE *awkwardly assumes the correct position.*

CU of their bodies close together.

CU TRUELOVE's *face, as if he's in pain. They dance on.*

Pull back to establish DUNDINE *looking at them.*

Mix to TRUELOVE *and* ROMELIA *leaving the dance floor.*

KEES *approaches.*)

KEES: I am going now, Neil. Do you want a lift?

ROMELIA: I can give you a lift if you want.

TRUELOVE: Well—great. OK, if . . . (*Looks around as if for* DUNDINE.)

KEES: Fine. Have you seen Lyndon? I think he's gone.

TRUELOVE: No.

DUNDINE (*approaching*): There you are. (*To* ROMELIA) Are we heading back? Can I hitch a ride?

ROMELIA: Sorry. I'm taking Neil.

TRUELOVE: Um look, Philip, it's OK with me, I don't mind if you . . .

DUNDINE: Oh no, no. Perish the thought, as they say.

KEES: You can come with me. I'm leaving now.

DUNDINE: Great. (*Frosty smile at* TRUELOVE) See you, Neil.
(*He walks away with* KEES.
CU TRUELOVE's *face. He looks as if he's about to say something.*)

ROMELIA: We can go?

TRUELOVE (*thoughtfully*): What? Oh yeah. Sure. (*They leave. We see a drunken* FFORDE *being helped out of the disco by* CONE *and* MURRAY. *The other boys drift away.* ROOTE *pauses to survey the bustling lively dance floor.*)

ROOTE: What a dump.

54. EXT. NIGHT. ROAD.

ROMELIA *and* TRUELOVE *on her Mobylette. They drive along.*
CU TRUELOVE's *face. His arms around* ROMELIA.
CU her hair being blown in his face.
She says something.

ROMELIA: You want some coffee? My house?

TRUELOVE (*shouting*): What?

ROMELIA: My house. (*She leans back.*) Do you want to come to my house for coffee?
(TRUELOVE's *face.*)

TRUELOVE: Yes. Yes please.
(*CU his face. He moves very slightly closer to her, marginally tightens his grip around her body.*
Her hair blows in his face.
He closes his eyes.)

55. INT. NIGHT. KITCHEN, ROMELIA'S HOUSE.

TRUELOVE *and* ROMELIA. ROMELIA *makes coffee.*
In this scene all the incidental noises—exhalations, rustles of
clothing, clinks, the noise of feet on the floor, etc.—are amplified
in order to simulate TRUELOVE's *intense sensitivity to what is*
going on, and his arousal.
ROMELIA: Sugar?
TRUELOVE: Please. Three.
  (ROMELIA *adds sugar.*
  CU her hands.
  The clear tinkle of the spoon as she stirs.
  Her face, profile. She turns.
  She hands TRUELOVE *the cup and saucer.*
  Their hands on the saucer, nearly touching.)
TRUELOVE: Thanks.
  (*Pause.*
  ROMELIA *smiles.*
  Brief CU of her lips parting.
  Brief CU of TRUELOVE's *eyes over rim of his coffee cup.*)
  Are your parents . . . ?
ROMELIA: Upstairs. Asleep. (*Looks at watch*) It's quite late.
  (*Pause.*) Ouf. It's warm. Don't you find?
TRUELOVE: No. It's . . . I'm OK.
  (ROMELIA *pulls her jersey over her head. She wears a*
  T-shirt, no bra beneath.
  The rustle of her clothes.
  Brief CU: her breasts.
  Brief CU: TRUELOVE's *eyes.*
  Whisper of her hair. TRUELOVE's *exhalation.*
  ROMELIA *smiles.*)
ROMELIA: What's your second name, Neil?
TRUELOVE: Oh. Ah, it's Truelove. Neil Truelove.
ROMELIA: Truelove? Like True—Love?
  (*She sings. Her voice, slightly amplified—as if sung close*

146

to TRUELOVE's *ears—is girlish, breathy and unbearably plangent.)*

ROMELIA: "While I give to you, and you give to me, true love, true love."

(TRUELOVE, *moved and embarrassed. Sets his cup down. CU of cup—its rattle against the tile surface.)* Like that?

TRUELOVE: Yes . . . unfortunately.

ROMELIA: But it's a good name. I like it.

TRUELOVE (*Pulling himself together*): Well, I've had to take a lot of crap about it at school. You know: "Lover-boy," "Lovey-dovey," "False Love"—that sort of thing . . . (*Pause.*) Childish . . . but just at school, that is.

ROMELIA: You like your school?

TRUELOVE: No. I hate it.

ROMELIA: You live there.

TRUELOVE: Yup. It's a boarding school.

ROMELIA: All boys? Together?

TRUELOVE: Worse luck, yeah.

(*Pause.*)

ROMELIA: For how long?

TRUELOVE: Oh. Ten years. I went when I was seven, you see.

ROMELIA: How terrible.

TRUELOVE: Oh no, it's quite common in Britain. (*Pause.*) Actually I don't hate it because I'm away from home. It's because at school you sort of feel that life is going on in the rest of the world, you know, that it's happening all around you and that you're kind of missing out on everything.

ROMELIA: I think that's awful. To be like that . . . You want more coffee?

TRUELOVE: No. No thanks.

ROMELIA: You want a biscuit? Hungry?

TRUELOVE: No thanks.

147

ROMELIA: I am.
(*She opens a cupboard and reaches to a high shelf.*
TRUELOVE *watches. As she reaches, her breasts rise and press against her T-shirt.*
TRUELOVE's *face.*)
ROMELIA: Can you get it for me?
(TRUELOVE *moves.* ROMELIA *reaches again.*
CU of an inch gap between T-shirt bottom and jeans top. The shadowed furrow of her spine. TRUELOVE's *hands reaching tin. He offers it to her. They are close. She puts tin down.* TRUELOVE *eases back. Brief CU of the shine of lights on her hair over noise of tin opening, rustle of paper.*
ROMELIA *offers tin.*)
ROMELIA: You sure?
TRUELOVE: Actually . . . no . . . (*swallows*) I won't, thanks.
(ROMELIA *bites into biscuit.*
Brief CU of her mouth: her tongue retrieving a biscuit crumb.
TRUELOVE's *face.*)
One good thing about school—the friends you make. You do make very, you know, *good* friends . . . without your friends you couldn't survive. We help each other get through, if you know what I mean. We have some good times. Some good laughs.
(ROMELIA *moves to put her cup down in the sink. This brings her quite close to* TRUELOVE. *They look at each other. She smiles.*
CU her eyes. He smiles back. They stand quite close for a while.
TRUELOVE *looks at the coffee in his cup.*)
Yeah. (*Clears his throat.*) We, um, have some good times. Good laughs. Couldn't . . . (*clears throat*) couldn't survive otherwise.
ROMELIA: I think I should take you back.
(*CU* TRUELOVE's *face.*)

56. EXT. NIGHT. VAN DER MERWE HOUSE.

ROMELIA *and* TRUELOVE *motor to a halt outside the front door.*

ROMELIA: Here you are. À *votre service.*

TRUELOVE (*deep in thought*): What? Oh. Yes. Thanks for the lift. And the coffee.

ROMELIA: Perhaps we can meet tomorrow?

TRUELOVE: No. I don't think so, we don't get back till late tomorrow.

ROMELIA: The day after, then. We can go to the disco again, OK? The evening of the day after tomorrow. We will meet there.

TRUELOVE: The day after tomorrow. Great. Definitely. (*Pause.*)

ROMELIA: He's a friend of yours . . . Philip?

TRUELOVE: Philip? Yes. Well, sort of my best friend, you could say.

ROMELIA: I see.
(*Pause.* TRUELOVE *inches closer.*
ROMELIA *smiles.*
CU TRUELOVE'*s face.*
Silence.)
It's late. I must go now.

TRUELOVE (*stepping back*): Right. Sure. The day after tomorrow, then?

ROMELIA (*starting bike*): At the discothèque. Good night.

TRUELOVE: Night.
(*He watches her go. Then he punches his palm furiously and admonishes himself silently. He gestures impotently at the night sky, then goes in.*)

57. INT. NIGHT. VAN DER MERWE HOUSE.

Very dark. TRUELOVE *creeping through the hall.*
Suddenly ANNA *steps out in front of him, a small white figure.*

ANNA: English boy!

TRUELOVE: Oh my God! (*He clutches his heart.*) Jesus Christ! (*Staggers from the shock he's received.*)

ANNA: Come here.

(*She takes his hand and leads him into the drawing room. She switches on a table lamp to reveal* LYNDON *comatose on a couch. On the carpet is a pool of vomit.*)

TRUELOVE: Oh God. Bloody hell.

(*They both stand and look at* LYNDON *for a moment. Then* ANNA *leaves the room.* TRUELOVE *shakes* LYNDON *awake and tries to get him to his feet.*) You stupid drunken cretin. Look what you've bloody done. Diced carrots all over the shop.

LYNDON (*coming around*): Oh Jesus. Oh God, Neil. My head. (*Groans. The room is flooded with light. They are discovered like two burglars. Cut to* MRS. VAN DER MERWE *staring in shocked disbelief at the scene,* ANNA *standing smugly beside her.*

TRUELOVE *and* LYNDON *look at each other.*)

58. INT. DAY. BUS.

Come in on a view of Amsterdam streets through the windscreen wipers of the bus.

Cut to MOLE, *wearing a beret and a smug expression on his face. In the seats behind* MOLE *we can see* CONE, ROOTE *and* DUNDINE. TRUELOVE *is sitting at the back beside* LYNDON.

ROOTE *leans forward to speak to* MOLE.

ROOTE: Excuse me, Sir.

MOLE: Yes?

ROOTE: Um, I—that's to say we—were wondering when we'd be getting our time off.

(CONE *and* DUNDINE *crane forward to hear the answer.*)

MOLE: Soon enough, Roote, soon enough. It's all arranged.

ROOTE: Arranged?

CONE: Can't we stop here, Sir, in the center? Canals, all that?

MOLE: No. I've a wee surprise.

ROOTE: We thought we were meant to be having some time off, Sir. In the city center . . . souvenirs, you know, Sir . . . My mother specifically asked me to get her a souvenir from Amsterdam, Sir.

MOLE: City center? Can't think where you got that idea from. (*Turns around.*) No, Roote. There's more to life than hockey matches and souvenirs for your mother. I've arranged a *real* souvenir of Holland for you. One that you'll treasure. One that may change your life as it changed mine . . . Ah, I think we're just about there.

(MOLE's *face lights up.*
Cut to the boys' faces: vast disappointment. Loud groans.
The bus stops.)

59. EXT. DAY. AMSTERDAM STREET.

The bus stops. It is still raining.
Pan from the bus to the Van Gogh Museum.
Pan back to bus.
The disconsolate, incredulous boys file off, MOLE *shepherding them.*

MOLE: This way. Over here. Stand here. Right, look lively now. All right, let's have you now. Come on—a lot to see. Lot to see. Come on, Jellicoe. Move it. Move it, son . . . Jildi, Mkwela. Jildi, jildi. Truelove. Right. Stand here. Wait here. (*He heads off up the steps to the museum entrance.*
Come in on TRUELOVE *edging diffidently up to* DUNDINE.
Beyond them we can see MOLE *approaching the door.*)

TRUELOVE: Hey, Phil. Guess what that moron Lyndon did . . . Boked all over the sitting-room carpet.

DUNDINE: Did he? Prat. (*Pause. Then, with fake indifference*) So how did you get on last night?
TRUELOVE: Oh, no go there. Just dropped me off.
(DUNDINE'*s face: slightest suggestion of relief.*)
DUNDINE: Ah well.
(*Amity is restored.*)
Yeah, well, I didn't like to say anything, but I could sort of see that . . . What is that idiot doing now?
(*Behind him we see* MOLE *fighting with the locked doors of the museum.*
CU MOLE'*s face: massive frustration, bitter disappointment.*
Cut to the boys all watching him.)
CONE (*super polite*): Excuse me, Sir, I think it's closed today . . . Sir.
(*CU* MOLE: *he shuts his eyes, bows head, touches his forehead against the door.*
He opens his eyes. Slightly manic stare.)
MOLE (*pointing*): Right. Up against the wall, you lot. Lamb, get my camera.
(*The boys all move reluctantly against the wall.* MOLE *erects his tripod, mounts camera and sets the timer. The buzz of the mechanism. He runs back and takes up his position in the middle of his team. The boys, behind him, play the fool.* MOLE *forces a smile.*
Click. Freeze frame.)

60. EXT. DAY. HOCKEY PITCH.

Come in on MOLE'*s feet in a puddle of water. Travel up* MOLE'*s body. It's still pouring with rain. The team—in soaking strip— stands in a miserable huddle on the edge of a complete mud bath of a pitch.*
MOLE *hectors them.*
MOLE: OK, so it's a little wet. A bit damp. (*Water runnels off his beret.*) But these conditions will suit us. These

guys are probably not used to playing in mud. (*He looks anxiously at his dispirited team*) Look, Mr. Ashbee has booked us all into some great restaurant in the city center after the match . . . Listen, if we win, I'll buy you all a drink. How's that . . . ?

61. INT. DAY. CHANGING ROOM.

Pan along the team, completely covered in mud, sitting glumly. MOLE *walks up and down the line, muttering as if to himself.* MOLE: Eleven-nil. Eleven-nil. Mmm. Eleven-nil. Uh-huh. Eleven-nil. Eeeeleven-nil. Hum. (*He exits. The team bursts out with laughter.*)

62. INT. NIGHT. BUS.

Bus moves slowly through winding Amsterdam streets. MOLE *and* FFORDE *sit together, toward the front.* MOLE *has a map of Amsterdam on his knee.*
MOLE (*philosophically*): You know, Fforde, life's a funny thing.
FFORDE: Sorry? What is, Sir?
MOLE: Life, Fforde, life.
FFORDE: What about it, Sir?
MOLE (*grim sagacity*): Do you ever . . . think about life, Fforde? You know: what it's all about, sorta thing? What its meaning is?
FFORDE (*in all seriousness*): Yes I do. All the time.
MOLE (*ignoring him*): Life is like a . . . like a map. (*Taps map*) Some of the streets are marked clearly—the route is obvious . . . But, in other areas, there's just a sort of dotted footpath . . . across a blank space . . . (*Gesture with hand.*) Terra incognita. Know what that means, Fforde?
(*Cut to* FFORDE, *barely listening.*)

153

Where you make your way, your weary way, along
the primrose path through the vale of tears as best you
can. (*Gesture with hand.*) And where—oh yes—*unlike*
the Psalm—the twenty-fourth Psalm—know the one I
mean, Fforde? You have *no* staff to guide you. No
rod, no staff . . . d'you see what I'm getting at,
Fforde? Can you sorta understand the significance?
FFORDE: But you're staff, Sir.
MOLE (*irritated*): What?
FFORDE: You're staff. And you're guiding us.
(*Cut to* MOLE, *flummoxed.*
The bus stops. CONE *comes down the aisle.*)
CONE: Driver says we're here, Sir.
(MOLE *looks out of the window.*)
MOLE: Don't be daft, boy.
MURRAY: Looks like the wrong sort of area to me, Sir.
MOLE (*standing up*): OK, everybody, off the bus. We'll walk
from here.

63. EXT. NIGHT. ALLEYWAY, AMSTERDAM.

MOLE, *looking lost with map in hand, leads his brood onward.*
CONE: I'm pretty sure you took the wrong turning back
there, Sir. If I could just have a look at the map,
I'm . . .
MOLE: Will you kindly shut up, Cone? Do you think I can't
read a map? (*Unconfidently makes a decision.*) Um, let's
go up this way. (*He leads them off in another direction.*)

64. EXT. NIGHT. SQUARE, AMSTERDAM.

MOLE (*worried*): Keep together, everyone, for God's sake!
Don't lose touch!
(*Cut to general panorama of the square: neon lights, clubs,*

154

cabarets. Cut back to CUs of various boys' wondering, astonished faces.)

MOLE: Keep calm! Eyes front. Don't panic. Stick together.

TRUELOVE: Oh my God.

DUNDINE: Here we go!

CONE: This is it.

ROOTE: You mean . . . ?

CONE: Got the money?

ROOTE: My God. Yes.

CONE: Let's go.

> *(They slip away and dart down a side alley.*
> *The other boys continue to follow* MOLE.)

MOLE: Stick together, lads, we'll be all right. We'll get through, don't worry.

65. EXT. NIGHT. STREET IN RED-LIGHT DISTRICT.

MOLE *leads the boys around a corner.*

MOLE *(counting)*: One, two, three, four, five, six, seven, eight, nine, ten. Ten. Ten. There's two missing. Oh, my God. Everybody stop. Stop! *(He scans the boys' faces.)* Cone and Roote. Bloody Cone and Roote! I'll kill them. Stay there, everyone. Don't move an inch. *(He dashes off in search.*
Cut back to the others, who survey the scene.
The classic Amsterdam red-light-area window: a bored and partially undressed TART *sits bathed in red light reading a paper. She looks up.*
Cut to the TART's *POV: the First XI, noses pressed to the glass staring in at her.)*

MURRAY: Jesus. She just sits there. You go in and . . .

SIMON: Like a sort of supermarket.

> *(Pause.)*

MURRAY: What do you think she's thinking?

SIMON: Search me.

(*Cut to the* TART *who stares impassively back at the boys.*)

MURRAY: Unbelievable.

DUNDINE: Christ, someone's just gone in next door!

(*As one man the team move over.*

Cut to the next window. A PUNTER *and* TART *look up, sensing they're being scrutinized. The* TART *comes over and peremptorily draws the curtains.*)

66. EXT. NIGHT. ALLEYWAY.

Cut to CONE *and* ROOTE *counting their money down a side alley. In this alleyway, the prostitutes more orthodoxly solicit from doorways.*

CONE: I've got thirty.

ROOTE: Twenty-two.

CONE: Fifty should be enough.

ROOTE: We'll be broke.

CONE: But it's worth it.

ROOTE: Fifty for the two of us.

CONE: You'll have to owe me a fiver.

ROOTE: Sure.

CONE: But I get first go as well.

(*They walk up and down the alleyway covertly inspecting the prostitutes.*) This one?

ROOTE: OK. Oh, my God.

67. EXT. NIGHT. ALLEYWAY, AMSTERDAM.

MOLE *searching for the boys.*

68. EXT. NIGHT. SIDE ALLEY.

MOLE *runs down alley, searching. Looks around. A very large, voluptuous prostitute in a window raises her eyebrows interrogatively. Her hand caresses a whip.*

MOLE's *face. He is horribly tempted. He takes two steps.*
Cut to PROSTITUTE. *She shifts her stance provocatively. Looks at*
him through lowered lids.
MOLE *adjusts his tie. He preens. His hand wanders toward his*
wallet. Suddenly he remembers his duty.
CU his face as lust and duty war furiously.
With a massive effort of will he wrenches himself away and
runs on.
PROSTITUTE *shrugs.*

69. EXT. NIGHT. RED-LIGHT STREET.

The other boys.
MOLE *rushes up, disheveled and panting.*
MOLE: Any sign?
FFORDE: No, Sir.
MOLE: My God, where are they? Little bastards. Lamb! Get
    away from that window. Back into the middle of the
    street all of you. Eyes on the ground, look at your
    shoes. Oh Jesus. Look at your feet. Examine your
    footwear. (*He dashes off again.*)

70. EXT. NIGHT. ALLEYWAY.

CONE *and* ROOTE *approach the* PROSTITUTE.
CONE: Right, you do the talking.
ROOTE: No, you.
CONE: Bloody hell, I'm lending you the money.
ROOTE: But you're having first go.
CONE: Oh Jesus, all right. (*To* PROSTITUTE, *who's been*
    standing listening) Evening. Speak English?
PROSTITUTE: Of course I do.
CONE: Um, right. Ah, us. You take us, yes? Two. (*Shows*
    money) For two. How much?
PROSTITUTE (*takes the money and counts it*): OK, you wait here.

(*She disappears into the doorway. Sound of her going
upstairs.* CONE *and* ROOTE *look at each other, transfigured
with excitement.*)

CONE: Sweet Jesus!

ROOTE: Hell's bloody bells.

CONE: You realize what's going to happen, don't you?

ROOTE: Christ. (*Pause. Then, strangled cry of triumph*) We've
done it, Coney! We've bloody cracked it, me old
mate.
(*They jump up and down doing a little dance of triumph.
Pause.*) She's taking her time a little bit, isn't she?

CONE: Probably getting the bed ready and that sort of stuff.

ROOTE: Oh yeah. Of course. (*Pause. Nervous laugh.*) I hope
she's not bunked off or anything.

CONE: Better not have.
(*Pause. They peer into the doorway.*)

ROOTE: Bloody hell. What are we going to do now?

MOLE (*VO*):Absolutely nothing.
(CONE *and* ROOTE *whirl around to find an irate* MOLE.)

71. EXT. NIGHT. RED-LIGHT STREET

Only LAMB *remains where the others were.*

MOLE *arrives pushing* CONE *and* ROOTE *before him like prisoners.*

ROOTE (*VO*): We got lost, Sir. We didn't know where we
were.

MOLE: I wouldn't trust you as far as I could throw you—
(*Notices* LAMB—*alone. Appalled*) Where is everyone?
Where the hell have they gone?

LAMB (*all innocence*): Er, I don't know, Sir.

MOLE: Right. Stay here, you three. If you move an inch,
I'll kill you. Dead.
(MOLE *races off into the crowds, a demented figure, in
search of the others.*)

72. EXT. NIGHT. RED-LIGHT STREET.

MOLE *darting in and out of porno shops, cinema arcades and strip club foyers, emerging with embarrassed schoolboys, herding them along.*

73. EXT. NIGHT. RED-LIGHT STREET.

MOLE *pauses for a moment, furiously writing in his punishment notebook. His back to a* TART's *window. The* TART *sits in her chair. Behind* MOLE, *in the* TART's *room, we see the door open tentatively and* THORNTON *with his case hesitantly advance. The* TART *looks around and gets to her feet. To her astonishment,* THORNTON *tries to kiss her. She slaps his face and gives him a shove.* THORNTON *falls over. The* TART *picks him up by the scruff of his neck and throws him out onto the street where he lands at* MOLE's *feet. The case thuds out beside him.*
THORNTON: Sir. Sorry, Sir. I thought I recognized someone I knew, Sir. Friend of my parents, Sir.

74. EXT. NIGHT. RED-LIGHT STREET.

Long shot of MOLE *herding and shoving the full team along the street.* MOLE *is demonic, possessed, a mad light in his eye.*
MOLE: Right. In file now. Move it there. Move it. Right along there. Come on now, Roote. Come on, let's have you. Don't just stand there, you scandalous little gerbils, you filthy little vermin . . . And you, Macgregor, you know damn well your father's a minister of the Church of Scotland. And you, Cone and Roote—another pair of young perverts. And Mkwela—your country should be ashamed of you. Murray—a nasty, nasty person. Oh yes, Dundine— another lovely couple . . . Truelove. Get a move on, Lamb . . .

(LYNDON, *bringing up rear, offers* MOLE *his bag of chips.*
MOLE *swats him over the head. Chips fall to ground.*)
Toe rag!
LYNDON (*contemplating chips*): Bastard.

75. EXT. NIGHT. BUS.

The bus traveling out of the red-light distict.
MOLE: . . . I turn my back for one minute and you're down
in the gutters swimming in the sewers with the filth.
(*Come in on* MOLE.)
Rats, horrible little rats, that's what you are. The
scum rises to the top, they say; well after tonight, I'm
not going to contradict anyone. Oh no. The scum
rises over the sinking ship, the rats are trying to leave
to join the alleyways paved with filth. Well, I tell you,
I know how to deal with rats. Rats don't get treated
like human beings. No, no, rats get treated like
rats . . .

76. INT. DAY. GUEST BEDROOM, VAN DER MERWE HOUSE.

*CU the window pane. Rain battering fiercely against it. Pull
back to show* TRUELOVE *looking mournfully out.* ANNA *plays in
the garden.*
Cut to LYNDON *still in bed. The room is in a shambles.*
LYNDON *wakes up, yawns, scratches. He looks revolting.*
LYNDON: What time is it?
TRUELOVE: Half-eight.
LYNDON: Right. (*Thinks.*) I'm off to the bog for a crap.
(*Gets out of bed, naked, puts on an old, verminous fur coat.*
He leaves.
Cut back to TRUELOVE.)

77. INT. DAY. LANDING, VAN DER MERWE HOUSE.

LYNDON *comes onto the landing through a door that clearly leads from a lavatory. He is naked underneath his fur coat. On the landing, he bumps into* MRS. VAN DER MERWE. *They jink to and fro until she flattens herself against the wall to let him pass.* LYNDON *moves out of shot.* MRS. VAN DER MERWE *goes into the bathroom. Hold on bathroom door for a second or two. Immediate sound of flushing.* MRS. VAN DER MERWE *bursts out of the door, leans weakly against the wall and takes a deep breath.*

78. INT. DAY. DINING ROOM, VAN DER MERWE HOUSE.

Come in on a CU of a doorstep of bread. Thick dollops of chocolate spread are being squeezed onto it from a tube. Pull back to establish LYNDON *at the breakfast table preparing a sandwich. Awkward silence from* MRS. VAN DER MERWE, ANNA *and* TRUELOVE. *On the table is the classic Dutch breakfast extravagance. Umpteen brands and types of jam, spread, chocolate, cornflakes, milk, yogurt, etc.*
LYNDON *can't resist this cornucopia. He adds some cheese to his chocolate, then some sliced gherkins topped with a generous sprinkling of coconut flakes. Puts the top on his sandwich and eats noisily and with huge satisfaction.* ANNA *looks on in disgust, pushes away her untouched cereal.*

79. INT. DAY. GUEST BEDROOM, VAN DER MERWE HOUSE.

The bedroom is a total shambles.
Both beds are unmade, clothes are scattered everywhere— LYNDON's *goal-keeping equipment is much in evidence.*
From downstairs comes the sound of loud rock music. TRUELOVE *walks around smoking, a little self-consciously.*

80. INT. DAY. LIVING ROOM, VAN DER MERWE HOUSE.

Come in on a weeping fig tree.
LYNDON *is idly picking leaves from the tree as he listens to loud music from record player.*
The front doorbell rings.

81. INT. DAY. HALL, VAN DER MERWE HOUSE.

LYNDON's *POV:* MRS. VAN DER MERWE *goes to answer the door. She opens it and we see* DUNDINE, *dripping wet. We hear their voices, faintly, as* LYNDON *might.*
DUNDINE (*oozing charm*): Hello, Philip Dundine. How do you do? Sorry to disturb you. I have a message for Neil and Lyndon.
MRS. VAN DER MERWE: Please come in . . . Neil is upstairs . . . Straight ahead at the top of the stairs.
(*Come in on* DUNDINE *as he removes his coat and hangs it up.*)
DUNDINE: What a beautiful house you have, Mrs. Van Der Merwe. Very, very . . . tasteful. Very.
MRS. VAN DER MERWE (*pleased*): Oh . . . Thank you. You are very kind.
DUNDINE: Are you an interior designer by any chance?
(*Cut to* LYNDON's *face: utter contempt.*
Cut to DUNDINE *who has paused at the doorway to the living room.* MRS. VAN DER MERWE *hovers in the background.*)
LYNDON: What do you want?
DUNDINE: I am the bringer of glad tidings: the match is off.
LYNDON: Fantastic.
DUNDINE: Rain stopped play.
LYNDON: So what are we meant to do?
DUNDINE: "Spend the day with our families," Mole says.
(*Indicates fig tree*) What happened here?

LYNDON: Oh . . . Winter.

82. INT. DAY. GUEST BEDROOM, VAN DER MERWE HOUSE.

TRUELOVE *still lies on the bed puffing at his cigarette. Then he hears the sound of footsteps on the stairs and leaps up in panic. He flings his cigarette out of the window and fans air into his mouth. He looks around the shambolic room in desperation.* DUNDINE *comes in.*

DUNDINE: Hi . . . Relax . . . Game's off. Rain.

TRUELOVE: Oh. Who says? Mole?

DUNDINE: Yeah.

TRUELOVE: How is he?

DUNDINE (*grinning*): Mad. Mad as hell.

    (TRUELOVE *grins back.*)

TRUELOVE: Some night, last night, wasn't it?

DUNDINE (*grinning*): Classic. (*Imitating* MOLE) "Rats don't
    get treated like human beings, oh no no no . . ."
    (*They laugh.*)

TRUELOVE: So what are we meant to do today?

DUNDINE: Hang around with our families.

TRUELOVE: Why don't we bunk off somewhere?

DUNDINE (*making a pained face*): My family have laid on
    some sort of "trip" unfortunately . . . (*Looks at watch*)
    In fact I'd better get going. Pain.

TRUELOVE: God. Me and Lyndon, all day. Wonderful.

DUNDINE (*looking serious*): Are you going to the disco
    tonight?

TRUELOVE (*briefest pause*): Yeah . . . well I suppose I might
    as well . . . Why? You're coming, aren't you?

DUNDINE: Yeah . . . No, it's just something I heard . . .
    (*CU* DUNDINE.
    CU TRUELOVE.)

TRUELOVE: What?

DUNDINE: Doesn't really matter.

TRUELOVE: Well, what? What is it?

DUNDINE: Something that one of the Dutch guys said about Romelia.

83. EXT. DAY. AMSTERDAM SQUARE.

High shot: LYNDON *and* TRUELOVE *descending from a tram. Cut to: the two of them crossing a street through the trams and the traffic.* LYNDON *is wearing his fur coat, and looks happy, enjoying the freedom.* TRUELOVE *is pissed off.*

TRUELOVE: Where the hell did you get that bloody hearthrug from anyway?

LYNDON: I bought it off Greetje's brother.

TRUELOVE: *Bought* it? God, he saw you coming . . .

LYNDON: Bloody doom merchant . . . Come on, cheer up. (*Gestures*) Look where you are . . . Die Nederland, Les Pays Bas . . .
(TRUELOVE *gives a rueful smile and follows him.*)

84. INT. DAY. CAFÉ, AMSTERDAM.

TRUELOVE *and* LYNDON *sit at a table in the narrow glassed-in terrace of a café.*

TRUELOVE *looks gloomy, preoccupied.*

LYNDON *plays with a ghastly mechanical souvenir he has bought (a clockwork windmill).*

LYNDON: Going discovating tonight with that Rumania?

TRUELOVE: *Romelia*, you peasant. No I'm not.

LYNDON: Oh . . . Why not?

TRUELOVE: Dundine says some old boyfriend of hers has turned up. A student.

LYNDON: Ow. Nasty one . . . But why don't you just come along anyway?

TRUELOVE: Well, according to Dundine, Romelia and this guy are pretty close, or something . . .

LYNDON: "According to Dundine" . . . I don't see why
you hang around with an oil like that. Classic *artiste du
pissoir.*
(TRUELOVE *looks at him as if to say: "You would think
that, wouldn't you?"*)
Forget the girl, forget the student. Just come along.

TRUELOVE: No. I'll just stay in. Doesn't seem much point.
I've got some booze left.

LYNDON: Suit yourself. (*Looks intently at* TRUELOVE.) But I
think you're being a right twat.
(TRUELOVE *takes this in for a moment, thinks about it, then
rallies himself. He speaks with little assurance.*)

TRUELOVE: I don't give a fish's tit for what you think.
(LYNDON'*s face, wry, sympathetic, looking directly at*
TRUELOVE. TRUELOVE *holds the gaze for a moment, gives a
sort of smile and looks away.*)
So much for the fabulous Dutch Girls.

85. INT. NIGHT. DISCO.

The disco is very loud and busy. Pick out ROMELIA *sitting at the
bar talking to some Dutch boys. Establish that the conversation
between the Dutch boys and girls is friendly and natural.
Cut to* DUNDINE *making his way through the crowd toward her.*

DUNDINE: Hi.

ROMELIA: Hello. How are you?

DUNDINE: Great. Absolutely great, I would say. Fancy a
dance? (*They move onto the dance floor.*)

ROMELIA: Where is Truelove? Isn't he with you?

DUNDINE: Neil? No.

ROMELIA: Is he coming later, with Kees?

DUNDINE: I don't think so. He said he was busy.

ROMELIA: It's strange. We arranged to meet here tonight.
(DUNDINE *shrugs and starts to dance.* ROMELIA *frowns.*)
And you're going tomorrow?

DUNDINE: Yeah, bright and early.
> (ROMELIA *takes a final look around. Starts to dance.*)

86. INT. NIGHT. DRAWING ROOM, VAN DER MERWE HOUSE.

CU television screen. The Gentle Touch *is on, dubbed into Dutch. Hold, then pull back to establish* TRUELOVE, MRS. VAN DER MERWE *and* ANNA, *all watching the show.* LYNDON's *ravaged tree is still starkly in evidence.* TRUELOVE *looks glazed with boredom.* ANNA *is fascinated by the show. Sound of a car outside. Then the front door opening. Nobody moves.*
The drawing-room door bursts open.
MR. VAN DER MERWE *enters holding* LYNDON's *fur coat at arm's length.*
MR. VAN DER MERWE (*aggressively*): Is this yours?
TRUELOVE (*standing up*): What? No, it's Lyndon's.
MR. VAN DER MERWE: You bring it into my house. It's
> filthy. It's full of fleas and bugs!
> (MRS. VAN DER MERWE *gives a little shriek of alarm.*
> *Conversation in Dutch between them.*)
MRS. VAN DER MERWE: Get it out of here, Victor, quickly!
MR. VAN DER MERWE: I told you that boy was an idiot!
> From the first moment I saw him!
TRUELOVE: Oh God. I'm really sorry. I didn't know.
> (ANNA *laughs delightedly.*
> MR. VAN DER MERWE *utters a throaty Dutch oath and marches out of the room. Camera follows him to the front door.*)

87. EXT. NIGHT. VAN DER MERWE HOUSE.

MR. VAN DER MERWE *steps outside and flings* LYNDON's *coat out onto the driveway.*

88. INT. NIGHT. DISCO.

Slow dance music.
CU DUNDINE's *hand as he slips it down* ROMELIA's *back to cup her bottom.*
Cut to CU of DUNDINE's *face, as he attempts to nuzzle her neck.*
Cut to CU of ROMELIA's *face: an expression of tired resignation.*
She pushes DUNDINE *away.*
ROMELIA (*patiently*): What are you doing? What are you trying to do?
DUNDINE: Christ, what do you think? I'm not here because I like the music, you know.
ROMELIA: Well, please stop, OK? If you want to dance, that's fine . . . (*She breaks apart.*) But I don't like all this little boy sexy stuff.
DUNDINE: Oh. Right. Very sorry, I'm sure.
(*She walks off.*
ROOTE *and his partner come by engaged in heavy pelvic grind. His and* DUNDINE's *eyes meet.* ROOTE *raises his eyebrows and makes a wry face.*
Cut to DUNDINE *who points at the retreating* ROMELIA, *makes a disgusted face and mimes "bitch."*)

89. INT. NIGHT. CAFÉ, AMSTERDAM.

MOLE, *in a cellar bar, consulting Anglo-Dutch dictionary, the better to order his drink. Writes on scrap of paper.*
MOLE (*consulting paper*): Ah . . . Ein jonge claere . . . alse du bliest . . . please.
WAITER: Gin? OK.
(MOLE, *disgusted, crumples up paper.*)

90. INT. NIGHT. DRAWING ROOM, VAN DER MERWE HOUSE.

LYNDON *and* GREETJE *on the sofa, kissing passionately. They are both drunk.* LYNDON *falls off sofa.*

91. INT. NIGHT. GUEST BEDROOM, VAN DER MERWE HOUSE.

TRUELOVE *in bed. Wakes up. Switches on light.*
LYNDON (*VO*): You take your brassière off first.

92. INT. NIGHT. DRAWING ROOM.

GREETJE: No. You take your trousers off.
LYNDON: No. You first.
GREETJE: No, you.
LYNDON: No, you.
GREETJE: No, you.
> (LYNDON *stands up.*)

93. INT. NIGHT. GUEST BEDROOM, VAN DER MERWE HOUSE.

TRUELOVE *in bed listening. He can't believe his ears.*

94. INT. NIGHT. DRAWING ROOM.

LYNDON *and* GREETJE *stand and kiss passionately.*
TRUELOVE (*appearing at door*): Jesus, Lyndon. What the hell's going on?
LYNDON: All right, Neil? How's tricks? Greetje's come to spend the night. Her folks have locked her out.
GREETJE: My parents, they don't like Lyndon, but I . . .
TRUELOVE: I can hear you at the top of the house, for Christ's sake. You can't do this, Lyndon. What if Mr. Van Der Merwe comes down?
LYNDON (*shouting*): Oh, sod him for a start. He was the shag who threw my fur coat out! (*He starts to take off his trousers, pulls them down to his knees.*
> GREETJE *starts to haul off her jersey.*)
GREETJE: Come on, Lyndon . . .

LYNDON: Oh Christ—all right, baby . . . here I come!
TRUELOVE: Oh no.
LYNDON: Yeehah!
TRUELOVE: For God's sake, Lyndon, listen to me!
(*The lights go on. They freeze.* LYNDON *stepping out of his
trousers,* GREETJE *on the point of unclipping her bra.*
Cut to the door.
The sleep-mussed VAN DER MERWES *look on in unabashed
horror and outrage.*
Cut back to TRUELOVE.
Covers eyes.)
Oh no.

95. INT. DAY. CLUBHOUSE.

MOLE *addressing the two teams and the parents.*
MOLE: Ladies . . . ladies and gentlemen. Mr. Ashbee,
    players and members of the Heemdaam Hockey Club.
    (*Suddenly lost for words. Then, grandly*) The sands of
    time have finally drawn to a close.
    (*Cut to the Dutch parents, implacable.*)
    . . . The curfew tolls the knell of our departure . . .
    (*Cut to team: sniggers.*)
    Or . . . or as we say in my own country: "Dinnae
    bide tae see aucht primsie brattle. A willie-waught
    strunts ony pattle." (*Hideous smile.*)
    (*Baffled Dutch parents, muttering among themselves.*)
    Thank you all for making us so welcome—even if
    you couldn't control the rain gods, ha ha—for what
    has been in the opinion of us all, a— (*The words stick
    in his throat. He loosens his collar. Forces words out in a
    curious grating voice*) a . . . most . . . successful . . .
    tour. Fforde.

FFORDE: Sir? . . . Oh yes. Ah, on behalf of the Strathdonald School First XI, I would like to thank the gymnasium . . . of . . . hockey, um gymnasium. Ah, club. Three cheers. Hip hip! Hip hip! (*Pause.*) Oh, sorry. Hip hip! (*The boys join in with their hoorays. On the last hooray,* THORNTON's *brown case bursts open, depositing an avalanche of lurid, shiny, sex "aids"—vibrators and pink Bakelite "things"—at the farewell committee's feet. He drops to his knees and shovels them desperately back into his bag.* MOLE *crouches madly beside him.*)

MOLE (*harsh whisper*): You animal! You disgusting obscenity!

THORNTON: Sorry, Sir. It was an accident.

MOLE: You dirty little weevil—your parents will hear of this!

ASHBEE (*handing* MOLE *a dildo*): Yours I believe, Sandy.

96. EXT. DAY. CLUBHOUSE.

The boys, laughing, smiling, make their farewells and go over to the bus and mill around loading up their gear, masking everyone's embarrassment somewhat. Then SIMON *looks up as if he's seen something in the distance.*
Cut to ROMELIA *and* GREETJE *crossing the playing fields.*

SIMON: Looks like Lyndon's tart. Who's the other one?

DUNDINE: Oh God, not her. (*He moves away.*)
(*Cut to* TRUELOVE.
Cut to ROMELIA. *She glances at him, but makes no move to join him.* TRUELOVE *hesitates. He goes over.*)

TRUELOVE: Hello.

ROMELIA: Hello. (*Waves one hand slightly.*) I came to say good-bye.
(TRUELOVE *looks around.*)

TRUELOVE (*bitterly*): Is your friend here?

ROMELIA: What friend?

TRUELOVE: Your "student." Your student friend . . . Philip
  told me.
ROMELIA: What student? What are you talking about?
  (TRUELOVE's *face. Suspicion dawns. He looks around, sees*
  DUNDINE *laughing in a group containing* CONE *and* ROOTE.
  DUNDINE *doesn't meet* TRUELOVE's *eye.*
  Back to ROMELIA.)
  Your friend. A very good friend to you, I think.
TRUELOVE (*suddenly worried*): Listen, you, ah . . . you didn't—
ROMELIA (*holds up hand*): Hey. Please.
TRUELOVE: Sorry. Very sorry. (*As if to himself*) Sodding
  two-faced little . . .
ROMELIA (*seriously*): I'm sorry. It's a pity.
MOLE (*shouting*): Right, everyone on board. Come on.
  Hurry up!
TRUELOVE (*a little desperately*): Look, I . . .
MOLE: Come on, Truelove. No time for long farewells.
  (*He taps him on the shoulder.*) Excuse me, young lady,
  but we have to catch a boat.
ROMELIA: Goodbye, Truelove.
TRUELOVE (*sensing his time is running out*): God, um,
  look . . . er.
MOLE: *Truelove!* Right away.
ROMELIA: Perhaps you can write me a letter?
  (*Their hands touch momentarily.* TRUELOVE *turns and gets
  on the bus.*)

97. INT. DAY. BUS.

TRUELOVE *standing at the front, looking at* DUNDINE *and others
at the back.* DUNDINE, *not catching his eyes.*
TRUELOVE *deliberately sitting on his own at the front, his face
tight and drawn. From his POV we can see* ROMELIA *waving.
Pull back to the others crowded at the windows, waving, blowing
kisses, making ad-lib rude remarks.*

98. EXT. DAY. FERRY.

The boys are grouped on the ferry. They are subdued.
TRUELOVE *stands slightly apart, brooding, dark.*
CONE: I mean, did anyone get off with anyone? I mean, seriously.
LYNDON: I did.
ROOTE: We all know about you, so shut up.
CONE: I got a few snogs, and that was it.
ROOTE: If only Mole hadn't interrupted us with that prossie.
CONE: God yeah. The bastard. He owes us fifty quid too.
DUNDINE: A complete waste of time.
CONE: Total disaster.
SIMON: Shambles.
MURRAY: So much for the Dutch girls.
ROOTE: Dutch girls! Don't make me laugh.
SIMON: Don't make me cry.
    (*Pause.*

    FFORDE *approaches. He looks appalling. His face is tear-tracked. In one hand he has a cigar, in the other a bottle of gin. There is a large damp stain over his groin.*)
ROOTE (*pointing*): Caught short, Giles?
FFORDE (*looking down*): Good God . . .
SIMON: Christ, Giles, you look pretty bad news.
FFORDE: Got three more bottles of this stuff. Having a little party, behind the purser's office. Bring your own fags.
    (*He sways off. The others start to gather up their bags.*)
MURRAY: Good God, poor old Giles.
CONE: Cracking up.
ROOTE: Cracked.
TRUELOVE (*approaching* DUNDINE): Can I have a word? For a sec.
DUNDINE: Hi, Neil. Sure.

(TRUELOVE *and* DUNDINE *move off inside the ferry.*)

99. INT. DAY. FERRY.

TRUELOVE *bitterly angry and trying to keep his emotions under control.*

DUNDINE: Bloody awful tour, wasn't it?

TRUELOVE: What do you mean by doing that, Dundine?

DUNDINE: Doing what?

TRUELOVE: You bastard.

DUNDINE (*feigning astonishment*): Jesus! What's the scene, Neil?

TRUELOVE: Don't come that. You know.

DUNDINE: Know what, for Christ's sake? What are you talking about?

TRUELOVE (*closes his eyes tightly for a second*): And to think I just sat there . . . while . . .

DUNDINE: Look, come on . . .

TRUELOVE: You handed me that pack of stinking lies . . . Wormed your way—tried to worm your way between us.

DUNDINE: Christ, steady on, man. (*Pauses, looks serious.*) I didn't want to have to tell you this, Neil, I really didn't. But . . . at the disco, she practically raped me.

TRUELOVE (*heavy irony*): Oh, yeah. Sure, *sure* . . . Just shag off, Dundine. I hate your stinking, frigging guts. (*Pointing at him, voice breaking*) Some bloody friend.

DUNDINE (*looking around, acting amazed*): I *am* your friend . . . Don't get so effing worked up, Neil. She's just a girl. You're not married to her or anything. Be objective: what does it matter? You wouldn't have seen her again.

(CONE *and* ROOTE *approach.* MURRAY *and* SIMON *behind. All carrying their bags. The others follow* FFORDE.)

CONE: What's going on here?

DUNDINE: Neil's all fired up because he says I ruined it with his Dutch tart.

ROOTE: Whor, you're *well* out of that, man.

DUNDINE: That's what I said.

SIMON: Right snotty bint, I thought.

CONE: A real ball-breaker, you know . . . Frigid.

TRUELOVE: How can she be a frigid ball-breaker?

CONE: Er, well, ah . . .

ROOTE: Look, you don't want to get in a fight over some girl.

MURRAY: Not worth it, old son.

TRUELOVE: It *is* worth it . . . From my point of view. It's a bloody disaster.

CONE: So join the club.

DUNDINE: It was all a mistake, Neil, that was all. (*Extends hand*) Honest. Look, I'm sorry. Come on, it's not worth it. Shake?

(TRUELOVE *looks at* DUNDINE: CONE *and* ROOTE, MURRAY *and* SIMON *gather around, hemming* TRUELOVE *in.*
TRUELOVE *looks around at them. He looks down at the ground.*)

CONE: Go on, Neil. Face it. Don't be stupid.

MURRAY: Don't be so bloody romantic.

SIMON: Don't be a wet pants like Giles.

(*Laughter.* TRUELOVE *and* DUNDINE *shake hands.* CONE *puts his arm around their shoulders.*)

CONE: Great. Now let's go and get well and truly zonked.

(*They begin to break up and move off.*
TRUELOVE *picks up his grip and passes* LYNDON.
TRUELOVE *pauses.*
LYNDON *is arranging chairs into a makeshift bed.*)

TRUELOVE: You coming, Lyndon?

LYNDON: No.

DUNDINE (*from doorway*): Come on, Neil. (*Exits.*)

LYNDON (*lying down on his "bed"*): I can't stand those
bastards.
TRUELOVE (*very surprised*): What? You mean . . .
LYNDON: Yeah. That lot. I hate them. No—not you. But I
do hate them . . . Look, Neil, if you want my advice,
just go your own way. (*Pause.*) Go on, Neil. I'll
see you.
(TRUELOVE *looks at him, then back at the doorway. He
pauses. CU his face.
Then he picks up his bag, takes hockey stick from it, and
goes out on deck.*)

100. EXT. DAY. FERRY DECK.

TRUELOVE *steps out onto the deck. He strides forward to the edge
of the deck and makes as if to hurl the stick into the sea.*
MOLE (*VO*): Truelove!
(TRUELOVE *pauses and looks up.
MOLE leaning over balustrade, back to his camera, where he
has set it up for another automatic shot. He glances around,
conscious of the whirring timer.
MOLE points at TRUELOVE.*)
Don't you dare, boy. Don't you dare.
(*Cut back to TRUELOVE. He looks at the sea, pauses, steps
forward as if to throw.
Cut to MOLE, timer whirring.*)
I'm warning you, Truelove. My word is law!
(*Cut to TRUELOVE. He has made up his mind.
He takes his stick in both hands then (slow motion), moving
to a clear patch of deck, he spins around and around like a
hammer thrower, building up momentum and throwing his
stick high and far out over the end of the boat.
Cut to MOLE.*)
My word is LAW!

(*Cut to* TRUELOVE.
Cut to the tumbling stick.
Click from MOLE's *camera.*
TRUELOVE *turns his face into the sun.*)

THE END